40
WAYS
TO TEACH
YOUR
CHILD
VALUES

40 WAYS TO TEACH YOUR CHILD VALUES

Paul Lewis

Tyndale House Publishers, Inc.
Wheaton, Illinois

Third printing, September 1986

Library of Congress Catalog Card Number 84–52798
ISBN 0–8423–0920–9

T   O   L   E   S   L   I   E
the woman I'm privileged to know as
friend, lover, wife, and parenting partner,
and the one who keeps flesh on the bones
of my great ideas. Shona, Jonathan, Shel-
ley, and David shall be blessed forever to
have known her as Mom.

CONTENTS

PART THREE: VALUES

ACKNOWLEDGMENTS

These forty lessons in parenting first appeared much as you find them here in the pages of *DADS ONLY*, a monthly newsletter for fathers, which I have edited since the fall of 1977. As one monthly edition led to another in this ministry to fathers, I turned to a number of talented friends for insight and help. The key ideas contained in fourteen of these chapters originated in the minds of ten knowledgeable individuals who responded to assigned topics and to whom I express my heartfelt gratitude.

Tim Hansel, president of Summit Expedition, sparked the chapter on courage. Psychologist G. Keith Olson, Ph.D., director of San Diego's Family Consultation Service, shaped the presentations on success, fear of failure, thankfulness, guilt, and the blues. Family counselor Mary Jo (Joey) Winter supplied the chapter on death. Psychologist Constance Adler, Ph.D., prepared the material on self-esteem. Pastor and counselor Gordon C. Hess helped with kids' rights. Child psychologist Les Carter, Ph.D., knew about keeping kids neat and clean. Humorist Craig Wilson wrote on laughter. Dr. Waylon O. Ward, director of Christian Counseling Services in Dallas, supplied "hidden messages." Author Richard J. Foster prepared the material on simplicity. And writer Phil Rawley opened the door on privacy.

All submitted to my editor's scalpel and frequent additions with uncommon grace. I remain in their debt.

I am also indebted to Paul Thigpen, the associate editor of *DADS ONLY* since July of 1983, who contributed skillfully to the updating of these chapters for publication.

And this father wouldn't still be in business if it weren't for the tolerant teenager, junior, preschooler, and infant named Shona, Jonathan, Shelley, and David, who live in his home, who have survived his parenting experiments, and who regularly put to rest any temptations he ever had to crawl on the fathering pedestal as the editor of *DADS ONLY* newsletter. Thanks, kids! It's much more comfortable down here.

—PAUL LEWIS, Julian, California

HOW TO USE THIS BOOK

You're not holding an ordinary book on parenting. And it could discourage you unless you understand how it was created to be used.

This book is intended to be a handbook—a kind of super-condensed, quick reference guide to forty of the most important skills, attitudes, and values your toddler, junior, or teenager will need to grow into a mature and successful adult.

The chapters are short. You can read any one of them in five minutes or less. So keep this volume handy where you'll spot it often and be reminded to read and reread sections as the needs arise.

Each chapter outlines the basic principles and practices that you as a parent should observe in order to instill successfully in your child an important life skill or understanding. So many succinct principles and practical ideas are packed into each chapter you can easily become frustrated, even discouraged, if you read several chapters at one sitting. So limit your intake to two or three at a time. Few parents—no matter how super or dedicated—can concentrate on more than two or three of these areas at a time. And even if you can, the overload will likely frustrate your child.

Here's the best way to use this book . . .

First, look through the Contents and pick two or three of the skills, attitudes, or values your child is now dealing with, soon will be, or about which you as a parent are curious. Then read those chapters.

Second, read with a pencil in hand. The key parenting principles in the chapters are identified by bullets. You may want to circle those that strike you as being particularly helpful. Each practical suggestion or activity is preceded by a box where you may check the idea you want to use. Some of the ideas will work best in one kind of parent-child relationship. Others will be best suited to a different mix of parent-child temperaments. Be sensitive to what feels most natural.

Finally, the Appendix of this book, "Keeping Track," offers a helpful way to chart your child's growth—the areas that still need development and those that have become pretty well mastered. There is a checklist of the forty skills, attitudes, and values this book covers. Write your child's name at the top of the checklist. If you have more than one child, additional checklists have been provided.

In this section, use the blank in front of each chapter listing to help you set priorities. Check the top two or three areas that currently concern you. Then, on the progressive scale after the chapter listing, circle the level to which you think your child has currently progressed in that area. Log his or her progress over a period of weeks and months, and when that category is well mastered, put a slash through your check mark to make it into an *X*, indicating completion. Then move on to other areas.

If all this seems too complicated or too organized to suit you, then skip it. If keeping track helps, great. Do it. The important thing. is to remain aware of your child's development as the weeks melt into months and years. Keeping problems from developing is much easier than repairing them later.

At the same time, knowing that you've thought through the important issues along the way and done what you could as a parent is the best defense you can make against the "guilties" that sooner or later plague every dedicated mom and dad.

Now, before you dive in, please consider these six truths effective parents must regularly review.

☐ *Realization One: Children ultimately make their own choices.* "Train up a child in the way he should go; and when he is old, he will not depart from it" (Prov. 22:6, KJV) is God's promise, but it is not a padlock on your child's ultimate freedom to exercise his or her own will.

Any child may disappoint you. Odds are that yours will at various times as he or she matures. But the parent who pays attention, works smart, communicates, and prays often will log many more joys than disappointments. It is important that your parenting self-esteem be rooted in the quality of your own dependent walk and confidence with God. Don't measure your parenting performance solely by how well your child complies with each of your preferences.

☐ *Realization Two: If you think you've largely failed so far, it is never too late to start doing what's right.* That is the wonder of God's grace. Even the worst of sinners can be forgiven and can gain a fresh start. Certainly, it's better to avoid trouble as a parent. And some problems, left unattended for years, may seem to defy rescue by even the most intense of efforts and fervent prayers. But no problem is ever beyond the reach of an omnipotent God. That alone is the reason never to give up.

☐ *Realization Three: Modeling is the bottom line.* If it were possible, parents would probably vote this principle out of office, much to their detriment. If allowed the luxury of saying one thing and living another, the dissonance in our lives and the burden of keeping a double set of books would drive us to insanity anyhow. Example is a difficult taskmaster, but no teacher is more effective. If the truths you value are to be etched deeply on your child, you must model what you preach.

☐ *Realization Four: No parent is an island.* The body of Christ principle applies in parenting as in everything else. As your child grows older there will be other adults who, because of their special gifts or positions of influence, will be able to break through with your child to present truths in ways you cannot. Instead of viewing this as a threat, take the initiative by watching for situations, even creating opportunities, where your child is exposed to other adults you admire. Suggest to those persons what you would like your child to learn from them and encourage them to take the initiative. Make the most of every opportunity.

☐ *Realization Five: A good marriage is more important in raising your child than excellent parenting skills.* Your child's sense of security is not rooted as much in your love for the child as in how much love he or she knows you and your spouse share.

Besides, what could be more important to a child who will one day establish his or her own marriage and home, than for you to demonstrate by your example that instead of getting divorced, a man and woman can live together, hold honest differences, work through even the thorniest of life's problems, and sustain an ongoing depth of mutual love and respect?

Certainly, God's grace can cover for mistakes. But avoiding the scar tissue is even better.

☐ *Realization Six: Kids forgive and forget much easier and longer than parents do.* It takes a lot of consistently negative experiences to sour your relationship with your child. So if he or she knows it is your deepest desire to be a fair and effective parent, your relationship can survive many mistakes without irreparable damage. When you've blown it as a parent, practice what you preach: say "I'm sorry" as sincerely and as quickly as you can.

Why are there boxes next to the six realizations listed above? So you can check the ones you most need to remember to become a more effective dad or mom. For in the final analysis, neither you nor your child can afford to stop growing.

One of the wonderful ironies of parenting is that we can't know how well we've succeeded in our assignment until it's too late. And just when our on-the-job training is complete, we're unemployed. All the more reason to pay attention, keep a good sense of humor, and give our children the best model to learn from that we can. The rewards are more than worth it.

After all, our children are the only possessions we can take with us to heaven.

PART ONE

SKILLS

Too often we give children answers to remember rather than problems to solve.
Roger Lewin

Determination to be wise is the first step toward becoming wise!
And with your wisdom, develop common sense and good judgment.
Proverbs 5:7, TLB

1

YOUR CHILDREN AND ALLOWANCES WHAT ARE THEY LEARNING ABOUT FINANCIAL RESPONSIBILITY?

TEACHING children the wise stewardship of resources is essential for Christian parents, and training them how to handle money is a good place to start. One of the best ways for children to learn about money is to have an allowance.

Many parents do not give formal allowances, but instead give their children money on an irregular, unplanned basis as it is requested. This method doesn't teach them how to manage money. Children must beg for money, and the parent must continually decide on the spot whether each request is legitimate and affordable.

A regular allowance avoids these problems, but there are widely divergent opinions about which type of allowance is best. Some parents pay children only for chores done around the house. Others give a regular allowance but withhold it if chores are left undone or as punishment for misbehavior. Many parents, however, think these methods encourage children to be good only for the money, and to see household chores as paid labor instead of natural responsibilities as members of the family. At the same time, the irregularity of payment makes it impossible for children to learn how to budget or save their income.

Other parents pay allowances regularly and at a fixed amount, with no conditions attached. This system seems best for helping children learn to budget, but it fails to teach the connection between work and rewards.

The best approach, perhaps, is a combination of these two methods. Give each child a regular, fixed allowance that must be budgeted for specific basic needs, plus a little more to spend at his or her discretion. This allowance is simply the child's share of the income as a family member. At the same time, basic responsibilities around the house are expected to be fulfilled; if they aren't, take disciplinary measures other than withholding allowance. In addition, extra chores you might normally pay someone else to do—like mowing the grass or washing the car—can be done by your child for additional earnings. This extra income will teach the connection between work and wages, and will be available to the child for "fun" things that aren't basic needs.

The effectiveness of such an allowance in building a solid sense of financial responsibility and values will depend to a great extent upon how much money is given and the guidelines you establish for its use. Here are some principles:

- The way you handle your own money is the strongest statement you will make, no matter what you say.
- Allowances should be paid regularly, on time, and without your having to be reminded. Regularity is the key to teaching discipline in spending.
- Advances on allowances should be rare. Give no more or less than what has been agreed upon so your child can learn to balance spending with income.
- The size of an allowance should be based on what the child is expected to accomplish with it, taking into consideration the child's age, readiness, and needs, plus the family's circumstances.
- Include a portion that can be spent however the child pleases so that he or she will learn how to make wise choices in spending.
- You are entitled to exercise some control to keep expenditures within the rules and values of the family.
- Don't use an allowance in place of your time or to "buy" love.

Here are some ways to help your child learn financial responsibility:

☐ Begin by helping your preschooler learn to understand pennies, nickels, and dimes in the context of playing store. Giving your child some change to spend on an occasional shopping trip with you will make the point that money is a medium of exchange.

☐ A young school-age child can be responsible for such items as lunch money, toothpaste, family gifts, and socks. Teach the importance of setting aside a tithe first. Then help the child to itemize on a budget worksheet the fixed expenses for which he or she will be responsible, as well as discretionary expenses. Also insist on some fixed amount for savings, preferably toward a long-term goal.

☐ Between the ages of seven and nine, most youngsters are ready to begin managing a weekly allowance using a budget worksheet. Items purchased with discretionary funds or savings will become especially important lessons in finance. As your child grows, he or she can save toward larger purchases. A few poor choices with this saved money will quickly teach the importance of price versus value. Let your child learn the hard way: don't bail him or her out, and bite your tongue when you want to say, "I told you so."

☐ Including a preteen in some family financial discussions is a good way for the child to learn that household income is limited, and that sometimes difficult decisions must be made about spending priorities. These family discussions can also become a good time for a child to learn about taxes, insurance, social security, and credit. Let your child help in decisions such as whether to buy a new car or to remodel the family room. Meanwhile, be sure that your child doesn't shoulder the weight of a financial crisis, or feel guilty about costing you money.

☐ Remember that as a child grows older, so does his or her need for money. A review of allowances twice a year is a good idea. A teenager should be encouraged to work outside the home, and this additional income should be deducted from the allowance so that the budget continues to balance. You can also help put a major purchase (such as a car) within reach and teach savings discipline by agreeing to put up one-half of the cost if the child will save the other half.

However you handle the details of allowances, remember: the best lesson your children learn about money will be your example. Are you modeling the priorities, values, and Christian stewardship you want your youngsters to learn?

2
DECISIONS
HOW TO HELP YOUR CHILD
MAKE GOOD CHOICES

DID you know that the decisions you made today were rooted in your own self-concept—that image developed over sixteen to eighteen years of growing up in your parents' home? How you view your ability to perform in relation to others substantially affects your decision making.

For that reason, helping children learn to make wise choices involves both teaching them an adequate process and helping them develop a healthy self-image of competence.

Although decision-making systems vary, the basic processes involved are defining the decision to be made, selecting the best option, and accepting and assessing the consequences. As a parent, your task is to model, guide, and support your child's developing competence in these processes, a job that will change as your child grows older.

☐ A preschooler sees you in a god-like role. He or she needs you to be directive without being dictatorial. You should help guide both the definition and selection phases of decision making. The child's greatest growth will occur as he or she realizes consequences and begins to apply what has been learned from past decisions. For example, you may be helping him or her decide which of two pairs of shoes is most appropriate to wear in cold or wet weather.

☐ During early childhood (ages six to eight), your child closely models you as his or her hero. At this stage, the child's participation in the selection process should increase. You can reinforce a positive self-concept by helping the child master certain tasks and develop a pattern of good choices in recurring decisions. How he or she spends after-school hours is a good opportunity to practice decision making.

☐ Preadolescents are beginning to sense that parents have both strengths and weaknesses. At this stage, a child's privacy and peer relationships will begin to divert more and more of his or her attention. So try to include the child's friends in some family activities. Help the preadolescent broaden significantly in decision-making skills by allowing him or her to assume responsibility to define alternatives and anticipate consequences. Keep your comments as suggestive as the child's maturity and wisdom will allow. Showing him or her how to list on paper the pros and cons of more complex decisions would be a good exercise. You may want to suggest six steps to follow in making a good decision:

1. Determine what needs to be decided.
2. Determine what the options are. Consider every possible way the decision could be made. Go beyond the obvious alternatives and consider more creative solutions. At this point, don't consider how "way out" the ideas may be; this is the time for brainstorming, and sometimes a crazy idea can lead to a practical one. Write down all ideas.
3. Think about the strengths and weaknesses of each choice. Now is the time to consider pros and cons, and to determine what is feasible and what is not. Search for all the possible consequences of each choice.
4. Choose the best alternative. If this first choice doesn't work out, make a second choice in the same way the first was made.
5. Do what you've decided to do.
6. Evaluate the decision after you've seen the results. Decide whether or not it was a good choice, and whether you'd make the same decision if you had to choose again.

In addition to these six steps, Joy Berry suggests three guidelines for the child to keep in mind in making every decision:

1. Do everything you can to show God your love for him.
2. Do everything you can to take care of yourself.
3. Do everything you can to show others you care.

For an excellent book to help children in decision making and problem solving, see Berry's *Making Up Your Own Mind* (Word, 1978).

☐ With adolescence often comes rebellious activity and tension. Be supportive as your child struggles to redefine himself. Encourage the teenager to build skills and develop talents rather than roles. Focus your attention on helping your child to clarify and define the decisions that must be made instead of evaluating the quality of his or her choices. Having to face the consequences of his own poor choices will be far more instructive than your strong words. The next stage will be complete independence.

☐ A good exercise for all ages is to role play a "what if" scene. Set up an imaginary situation—as common or unusual as you like—and ask, "What if this happened to you? What would you do?" Then go through the decision-making process together. Try situations like these: What if you missed your bus stop and found yourself in a strange section of the city without money for a phone call? What if your best friend asked you to help him or her cheat on a math test? What if someone asked you to marry him/her? What if you were graduating from high school and had to choose a college?

Throughout the process of learning to make decisions, don't force or even encourage leapfrogging of the stages. It will only frustrate your child and require relearning later. Give a positive model in the way you approach decisions in the family. Your child will be watching. Admit your mistakes and celebrate your successes. And remember, your basic assignment as a parent is to work yourself out of a job.

3

FINDING TIME
DOES YOUR CHILD
KNOW HOW?

TEACHING your child to manage his or her time probably isn't first on your list of priorities, if it is there at all. But maybe it should be.

As adults, most of us recognize that good time management

habits are the key to finding time for all the extras that make life fun and rewarding. And that's true for children, too. The more time efficient they are in straightening their rooms, performing chores, doing homework, and taking care of other "givens," the more time they'll have for hobbies, reading, enjoying friends, and all the other activities that will enrich their lives.

- In helping your child, remember that time management and a sense of responsibility come more easily to some children than to others. Be sensitive as you lead your child from one level of ability to the next.
- Establishing priorities is probably the key facet of time management. Seldom does anyone, even a child, have enough time to do everything he'd like to do. Consequently, value judgments will play a critical role in a child's time management decisions. And helping your child build a growing pattern of good choices is important. The child will get good at what he or she practices.

Here are some practical suggestions for each age level:

☐ Obviously a preschooler's ability and need to manage time are quite limited. This carefree age shouldn't be unduly cluttered with the pressures of time. A child's perception of time grows slowly. It's more often measured in terms of "how many nighttimes" till Grandpa and Grandma come to visit, rather than minutes, hours, and days.

☐ As your child is ready, you can introduce a sense of time efficiency by setting a timer for him or her to race against in picking up toys or performing some other chore. If the child is losing too often, pitch in at the last minute and help so he or she doesn't become discouraged.

☐ A family activity such as cleaning up the yard together can be a good way to build a sense of time values. Set a time limit for completing the work and offer a reward everyone will enjoy if the work is done in time. Outline the points of progress along the way so that everyone can pace himself and see how well he is doing.

☐ Most elementary-age youngsters can tell time and will profit from wearing an inexpensive wristwatch. A colorful calendar in a child's room can also help him or her follow larger chunks of time. During the school year, help your child create a time chart showing each hour of the day for a week. Then encourage the child to record throughout the week how he or she is spending those hours. At the end of the week, help your child add up the number of hours spent on each activity.

Next, your child should look at the completed chart carefully to find out how he or she spends time. Have him or her answer these questions:

1. What did I spend the most time doing this week? The least time?
2. What things would I rather spend more time doing? Less time?
3. What would I like to have done, but didn't?
4. Did I have enough free time to do what I wanted to do?
5. Do I feel good about how I spent my time?

Now block out on paper together how the child is going to budget the hours between school and bedtime each evening to reflect his or her priorities and goals. Plan together time for homework, chores, play, music lessons, or other needs and responsibilities. Your child will quickly discover that doing the "givens" efficiently is the key to having more time to use any way he or she wishes.

☐ During the summer, suggest that your child list activities to do, things to learn, friends to have over, books to read, and other goals he or she has in mind. Then give your child a calendar and help him or her assign the goals to specific weeks and days over the course of the summer. Allow plenty of slack. If the child marks an *X* through the days as they pass, he or she will discover whether time management habits are adequate for his or her goals.

☐ Be careful that your youngster doesn't get under the burden of failing. When you notice him or her constantly wasting time, a gentle reminder about the goals he or she set can be appropriate. And providing some reward for meeting the goals can help if your child is tempted to abandon them. Another good way to motivate is to team up two or more children to help each other reach personal or group goals. Nothing breeds a sense of progress and self-esteem like success.

☐ As a child moves into preadolescence and teenage years, time management skills become both more crucial and more difficult. Planning a basic weekly calendar of activities and responsibilities is important. It should reflect mature priorities and allow for a balance of work and play, as well as social and spiritual development. Show the child how to budget time ahead for major tests and term papers at school. Determining ahead the best use of a given slot of time helps overcome the temptation to blow time or lose it through indecision.

☐ You may also want to help your teenager plan long-term strategies for use of time. Talk together about weekly, monthly, and even yearly schedules for long-range ambitions.

As you seek to impart good time management skills, keep in mind that you must model what you teach. Time can't be stored—so what better moment than now to begin teaching its value and proper management?

4

ON LEARNING THE
ART OF FRIENDSHIP

AMONG the essential skills of
living, few are more crucial than understanding how to build
and preserve good friendships. Both with God and with those
around us, friend relationships are the stuff from which we
carve self-worth and a happy life. They impact enormously our
personal development, and are the glue that bonds strong families together.

But what characterizes the art of making and being a friend?
And how will your child learn it? Both sociological research
and common sense suggest that it begins largely with what you
model as parents—the qualities of friendship your child observes in how you and your spouse treat and respond to each

other. How do you handle your conflicts and express your joys? Does your child sense that you are best friends?

But modeling isn't the only way you can teach your child about friendship. Here are some other ways:

☐ Your child's first six years are spent moving toward a sense of healthy separation from his or her parents, especially Mom. The focus for these years is on mastering him or herself and the environment. Friends are seen merely as parallel travelers, which explains the child's frequent disregard for the interests of others. During this time, your child's need to possess must be satisfied before genuine sharing can take place. Self-centeredness must gradually give way to concern for others.

☐ While preschool is an excellent laboratory for learning which responses to natural inclinations are acceptable, you can also be dynamically involved in the process. Take your three- or four-year-old on an outing with two or three friends. Notice his or her verbal and physical expressions of selfishness. Then, in a gentle, positive way, offer some ideas for alternative behavior. Play is the primary context at this age for learning good friendship skills.

☐ As your child's comfortableness with autonomy grows, so will his or her attachment to others. During the elementary-age years, talk together frequently about his or her friends. Help your child express what those friends are like, and what they like to do. Make up adventure stories and draw pictures that include these friends. Begin now to talk about the negative results of choosing poor friends.

☐ Playing cooperative games helps build essential skills. Invite friends along on family outings and over for dinner. Take your child shopping for friends' birthday gifts, or help him or her make a simple toy, game, or craft as a gift. While you shop or work, talk about the feelings of affection you feel for various people you know, both within and outside your family.

☐ In the preadolescent years, your child's focus on relationships will move more to peers of the same sex and to adults outside the family. This "gang" helps him or her learn feelings of belonging, and the confidence of having something valuable to offer. Scouting and other children's organizations are also healthy expressions of the desire to belong to a group.

☐ During these preadolescent years, help your child grow in self-confidence and a better understanding of him or herself through outings, slumber parties, and overnight visits with friends. Short vacations with another family or group can be great fun. Your child's ability to stand alone when necessary in adolescence will be built on a foundation of being liked by friends. Understanding the kind of friends that should be chosen must be a continuing goal.

☐ You may need at times to help your child evaluate and curb those friendships that are having a negative influence. And you'll likely need to help your child learn to appreciate and include in his or her circle of friends someone he or she doesn't see as likeable.

☐ Throughout these preteen years, you are your child's sanctuary from those who reject his or her friendship. You also continue to be his or her model for reaching out to others. Be sure to talk with your child about the basic qualities of good friendship, such as listening and being interested in others, seeking them out, appreciating and praising their good qualities, sharing feelings, and keeping confidences.

☐ In the adolescent years, children are moving through a self-reevaluation process, initially through group participation and acceptance, and later through more individual and independent actions. During this period of your child's growing maturity, you have opportunities to express unconditional acceptance and to model adult qualities of true friendship. This must include transparency, the taking off of the mask worn to hide your true feelings from others.

☐ Take time to explore your feelings and those of your child. Discuss and list the qualities you look for in a friend. Prioritize these and evaluate your current relationships in light of these lists. Recognize together that friendship involves both giving and receiving. Spend time demonstrating to each other the key friendship qualities of communication, advice, praise, loyalty, and trust. Talk also about the unpleasant side of friendship, such as jealousy, deciding between two friends, apologizing, and the death of a friendship.

☐ If at this point you and your child aren't true friends, take steps to restore the relationship. This must begin with a genuine humbling, forgiveness, and reconciliation. These are the tough moments of friendship when wrong must be admitted and the truth spoken in love. Once healing has begun, talk about the fact that in the face of difficulty, the most common pattern (unfortunately) is to dissolve the relationship rather than work through the problem.

Your child's skill at initiating and nourishing good friendships will depend on large measure on the modeling and learning experiences you provide. It's a great responsibility, but the happy fruit is a lifelong treasure of knowing your child as a genuine friend.

5

EXPOSING YOUR CHILD TO POLITICS

WHAT should your child know about politics? In a time of growing plurality in viewpoints and a cancerous suspicion of politicians, it is essential that your child develop a genuine understanding of the political process in this country, and a commitment to see it work well. *We* are the government—not "those politicians." And what better time than now to instill this fundamental principle?

At the heart of healthy political convictions is a patriotic spirit—a persistent appreciation for this country and its historic commitment to human freedom and dignity. This can include affirming America's Christian heritage. George Washington said, "It is impossible to rightly govern the world without God and the Bible." Clearly Christian values underpinned the good sense our founding fathers used in framing our system of government.

At the same time, genuine patriotism recognizes a nation's past mistakes, present shortcomings, and possible future pitfalls, and it desires to right those wrongs. To love our country is to want to make it more just and compassionate—and that's why patriotism should lead to involvement in the political process.

Here, then, are some ways to build an appreciation for our heritage and an enthusiasm for actively preserving it:

☐ On national holidays, such as Memorial Day, the Fourth of July, Columbus Day, and the birthdays of national leaders from our past, gather the family, salute the flag, and offer prayers for this nation. Pray especially for our leaders.

☐ Periodically in family conversations or en route to church, talk about the precious right of freedom to worship. Discuss what it would be like to live in those countries that deny this basic right.

☐ Expose your child to objective biographies of America's founding fathers and great leaders. Avoid those books that praise their subjects uncritically, as well as "mudraking" biographies, intended solely to discredit our national heroes.

☐ As you read, clip or copy quotes from books, magazines, and other literature that state well the principles and values you believe in. Compile these in a scrapbook, and on special days of the year, share them with your child and discuss their meanings. Both the scrapbook and the discussions will become an important addition to your child's personal heritage.

☐ Make a practice of conversing about the day's news at the dinner table. Try assigning your child a dinner news report, summarizing the news from the front page of the paper or from the evening broadcast. As he or she reports, be persistent with the question, Why? It will help him or her probe behind the information to the basic causes, implications, moral issues, and historical significance of the events.

☐ Sort through various biases in attitudes toward government.

Talk about the meaning of labels such as conservative, liberal, and radical; left and right; Democrat and Republican. Look beyond the labels to consider together the basic attitude of a political viewpoint: Is it rooted in the humanistic view that man is good and capable of solving his problems without God? Or is it compatible with the biblical view that man is basically sinful, which limits what government can do in achieving ultimate solutions?

☐ As you come across biased reporting or fallacious thinking, involve your child in drafting a letter to the editor or manager of the radio or TV station that carried the report. The exercise will sharpen both your mind and the child's in thinking through issues and forming creative alternatives.

☐ Make it fun to learn the names of elected officials representing you on the city, county, state, and national levels. The *My Country* game in the *Laugh & Grow* series (Serendipity House) is a helpful tool in this regard.

☐ When the value of governmental controls is questioned by your child, talk about the consequences of not having a health department, public school system, or street maintenance department. A visit to or a discussion about a foreign country where these benefits don't exist quickly builds a respect for America. Also point out what happens when bureaucracies in America become too powerful or mismanaged.

☐ Take your child to a political rally. Afterward, discuss what happened and what was said.

☐ In the teenage years, involve your child in the political process on some level. Precinct canvassing with handbills in your neighborhood is a good place to start. Contact your local party headquarters. Learn the name of your precinct chairman. Then volunteer your help. If there is no chairman, consider doing it yourself.

☐ Help with the telephone canvassing for a candidate you support. The exposure to divergent points of view will test and strengthen your beliefs and perceptions of the issues, and help you discuss them more clearly with your child.

☐ On your next vacation, visit the legislative chambers of your state capitol. Or watch on TV the U.S. Senate or House of Representatives proceedings. Help your child interpret what's going on.

☐ With your child watch televised portions of our national political conventions. Talk about the importance of what's going on, and look for biases in the speeches or reporting.

☐ Join and support financially as a family those causes and candidates that take a morally correct stance. Taking an activist's position speaks volumes to your child.

With a little creativity and imagination, exposing your child to politics can be both fun and rewarding. Never in the history of our nation has it been more important to raise a generation of motivated and perceptive citizens. The process will happen one home at a time.

6

HELPING YOUR CHILD
COPE WITH GUILT

ONE of our goals as parents must be to help our children develop strong and healthy consciences. They must gain an understanding of guilt by learning the difference between the "fact" of guilt and the "feelings" of guilt. Feeling guilty does not always means a real transgression has occurred.

An imbalanced perception of guilt may have one of two unhealthy results. A person may suffer from the oppression of a cruel, tyrannical superego that cannot distinguish between genuine and irrational guilt. Or the very opposite problem may result: he or she may be capable of doing wrong without any apparent feelings of guilt at all.

In training our children, it is important that they (as well as we) distinguish between factual guilt and false guilt. Both are usually accompanied by guilt feelings that are unpleasant. But guilt feelings from genuine guilt can motivate us to repent and be forgiven, while false guilt feelings only haunt and slowly destroy us.

1. *Factual guilt* is the result of an actual violation of civil or moral law—what the Bible calls sin. When Mark comes home from junior high school feeling empty and sullen because he cheated on his math test, he's experiencing negative feelings from factual guilt.
2. Guilt feelings that come from one's failure to gain the approval or praise of others are the result of *false guilt*. When six-year-old Susie falls on the playground and feels rejected and stupid because her friends call her a baby for crying, that's false guilt.
3. Feeling guilty for falling short of one's own unrealistic expectation is another kind of false guilt. A typical example is when Jimmy is ashamed and embarrassed because he struck out in the bottom of the ninth with the bases loaded.

Too often children struggle unsuccessfully with persistent guilt feelings because they can't pinpoint the source of their guilt and thus can't deal properly with it. Each of the three kinds of guilt feelings described above requires a different approach.

Mark's factual guilt, for example, will be removed when he admits to himself that what he did was clearly wrong, confesses it to God and then to his parents and/or teacher, becomes willing to take the consequences, and makes a personal commitment not to repeat the wrongdoing. In the Bible this is known as repentance, and each of these steps is necessary to remove the feelings of factual guilt.

Young Susie's feelings of guilt for crying will go away when she is encouraged to give herself permission to cry when hurt, even if others do make fun of her. Children need to offset their sensitivity to their peers' approval or rejection with a growing trust in their own perceptions and decisions.

Jimmy's guilt feelings will vanish when he admits to his unrealistic expectations. He is his own worst critic and desperately needs from his parents unconditional love and acceptance that is not altered or lessened whenever performance is less than perfect. Unconditional loving, more than anything else, helps a child see himself as a special and valuable creation of God.

Here, then, are some important ways you can help your child gain a balanced skill in coping with his or her guilt:

☐ Avoid intensifying guilt by telling the child what a bad person he or she must be to have done such a terrible thing. Emphasize that the behavior is bad, not the person. "Hate the sin but love the sinner."

☐ Never withdraw your love and affection as a form of punishment. Let your love reflect God's love, which is unconditional despite our failings.

☐ Match the intensity of your discipline to the severity of the transgression, not to the intensity of your emotional displeasure. If you must, give yourself time to cool off before administering correction.

☐ When disciplining, always provide a way for your child to retain his or her sense of value and dignity. Don't accompany correction with angry accusations or insults to the child's character or worth, such as, "You're just lazy!" or "You always make stupid mistakes!" And don't humiliate him or her in front of others.

☐ Structure your child's chores, responsibilities, limits, and rules in a way that optimizes his or her chances for success. Keeping the expectations in line with the child's level of maturity protects him or her from the tyranny of unrealistic goals and excessive disappointment.

☐ Be alert to reading materials, TV shows, movies, and real-life experiences that demonstrate healthy attitudes and solutions to guilt. Help your child understand the situational ethic, which underlies most of our culture's false view of right and wrong.

☐ When your child describes the misbehavior of a peer, capture the usefulness of the moment by asking, "Was that wrong?

Why?" You'll gain a window on your child's thinking and understanding of guilt.

☐ Model in your own life a proper response to the three kinds of guilt feelings. There is no more effective way to teach. And when your child observes and confronts you with wrong-doing in your life, openly accept it as a golden moment of growth for both of you. Let him or her observe your repentance as well.

☐ Forgiving your child and teaching the art of forgiving others will also increase the child's capacity to forgive him or herself.

You can give your child few greater gifts than an understanding of the sources of guilt and the ability to deal with them. Such a well-informed conscience will become the root of a happy, healthy life of obedience to God.

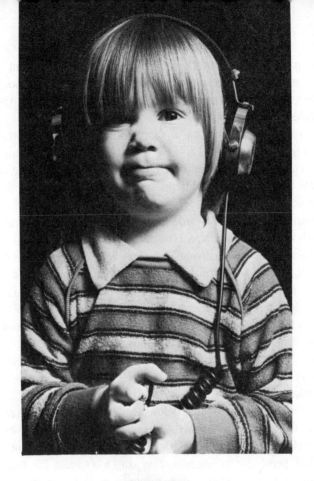

CAN YOUR CHILD DECIPHER
HIDDEN MESSAGES?

THE way we sit or look, the way we feel, what we say, and what we don't—everything about us communicates a message. Research reveals that only 7 percent of personal communication is verbal. Of the rest, 38 percent is tone of voice and 50 percent is from nonverbals such as body language. So it is crucial that children learn to interpret the hidden messages directed their way.

Younger children have a natural ability to sense parental feelings, but they tend to take words literally. They can also become confused when a person's body language and tone of voice are conveying a different message from what he or she is saying.

One day Waylon O. Ward's first-grader, Tim, came home from school crying. Tommy, a classmate, was a bully and liked to trip and kick Tim. In drying Tim's tears, Waylon's wife explained that Tommy was probably lonely, without many friends, and was doing this just to get attention. She proposed that Tim invite Tommy home after school the next time he acted mean.

A few days later when Tommy kicked again, Tim had a new interpretation of the event and thus a different response. He said, "Tommy, let's be friends. You want to come to my house after school?" It was the beginning of many pleasant experiences together.

Most experts agree that before age ten or so, children have no ability to think abstractly. When accidents happen, for example, they frequently need help to understand they're not a "bad" person for spilling milk or breaking a keepsake. The anger we may show as an immediate response on such an occasion—especially through a glance or other nonverbal cues—can be devastating to a child.

Such anger is one of the most common hidden messages. We'll often deny it with our words but confirm it in our emotions and nonverbals. Once a parent's anger is sensed, no amount of reassuring words can erase a child's frightened and unloved feelings. A far better approach is to admit your anger and assure your child that he or she is still very much loved. Acknowledging true feelings serves to verify what the child "heard" nonverbally and relieves much of his or her fear.

Often parents use hidden messages to manipulate children. We get that "hurt" look when a child does something we don't like. It isn't until much later in life that a child may come to recognize this behavior as the source of pent-up feelings of guilt and anger. When we catch ourselves manipulating in this way, we need to admit it openly and apologize.

As children move into preteen years, their ability to do more rational and abstract thinking improves. They are better able to interpret hidden messages. In fact, this heightened ability to read a parent's feelings and attitudes nails us when we're inconsistent. For example, we often offend youthful idealism when we affirm the importance of church on the one hand and pick apart the pastor's sermon on the other.

Whether it's with clothes, music, or whatever, you can encourage a healthy relationship when opinions differ between you and your teen by clarifying honest expressions of opinion: "Son, I realize this is only my opinion. Would you like to disagree?"

Some specific guidelines to remember regarding hidden messages are these:

☐ Touch is perhaps one of the most important facets of nonverbal communication. Children need hugs, pats, and other messages of affection, especially after discipline has been administered. Even if your words must be firm or correcting, your touch will reassure your child of the love behind the discipline.

☐ Take note of your tone of voice and facial expressions when speaking to your child. Ask yourself what these messages are saying, and whether they agree with your words.

☐ Clenching hands, twisting rings or hair, doodling, pulling at buttons or jewelry, or looking around the room all indicate unspoken feelings and attitudes, such as nervousness, boredom, or anger. Be aware of these cues in yourself and in your child.

☐ Help your family learn to interpret silence—it can express a number of feelings, from anger to grief to shock. If you think your child may misinterpret your silence, use a few words to clarify your feelings. For example, if you are silent because your concern for a sick relative is occupying your thoughts, explain that is the case so your child won't think you're angry at him or her for some unknown reason.

☐ Help your young child interpret daily events and his or her own feelings in response.

☐ Make a game of exposing the hidden messages in advertising slogans and images on TV and magazines.

☐ Apply the listening and identification skills you gain to your own family communications. Encourage candor. Ask your spouse to help you be more aware of the feelings and messages you are communicating.

☐ Model consistency in communication. Acknowledging your true feelings, even when they're not what you want them to be, is essential if your child is to become adept at doing the same.

☐ Avoid coercing your child into trying to feel what the child thinks he or she ought to feel. This only causes inconsistency in the child's communication.

☐ When your child calls your hand on a hidden message, admit it. Honesty is much less frightening than a contradicting hidden message.

Clear, complete communication can be a hallmark of your family's way of life—if you care enough to help each other listen for the whole message.

8

FINANCE AND ECONOMICS YOUR CHILD CAN UNDERSTAND

LIKE everyone else, children are impacted by inflation and economic uncertainty. Things they want to do and buy often cost too much, especially when a sagging economy reduces their parents' income or even puts them out of work.

Unfortunately, the causes of these economic realities often remain obscure to children. And when no one helps them gain an understanding of economics before they leave home, it is little wonder that counselors cite financial problems as a root cause in 90 percent of the divorces they see.

But it can be different for your child. With a little help, even a seven-year-old can begin to grapple with some of the basics.

☐ A good starting point is to teach some economic principles. Ask your child, for example, to guess what would happen if ten kids on the block each had a lawn mowing service, as opposed to only one kid looking for lawn mowing jobs. In the resulting dialogue, introduce names for the key ideas, such as marketable skills and the law of supply and demand. Show how these affect price and job availability. Be sure to talk about the motivational differences between being paid by the job and being paid by the hour.

☐ Once these basics seem clear, move on to discovering why work is necessary. Using your own job as an example, explain that God wants parents to provide food, shelter, and clothing for the family (1 Tim. 5:8). Look through some *National Geographics* or similar magazines together and observe how work is a part of every culture. As the contrasts in living standards and opportunities among nations become obvious, discuss the differences in opportunity created by various natural resources and political and economic systems. Keep the discussion at your child's level of understanding.

☐ It is likely the observed inequities will also generate an ideal backdrop against which to discuss the uses and abuses of welfare. After reading 2 Thessalonians 3:10 and Matthew 25:14-19, 36-40, pose a question such as this: "With what you now understand about work, pay, welfare, and the privileges of membership in this family, would it be most fair for you to be paid for doing all chores, some chores, or none of the chores?" Enhance the application further by having the child list the various tasks he or she does alone or with help, both daily and weekly.

☐ When you've reached agreement about which chores are to be paid in your family, use the moment to discuss how pay relates to skills, time, and efficiency. Calibrate chores according to their frequency and difficulty, and write a contract outlining the amounts and terms of payment to your child.

☐ If your child is old enough to grasp more about work, the

marketplace, and handling money, help him or her select and plan a simple business. It could be anything from a summertime lemonade stand to more unusual efforts such as a newspaper clipping service, birthday cake baking, or various other kinds of services like car, yard, or home cleaning. Forty-six good ideas are included in Malcolm MacGregor's helpful book, *Training Your Children to Handle Money* (Bethany House, 1980).

☐ Once money is earned, your child is ready to tackle management skills. Create together a simple budget that helps forecast how the money should be spent. Budget categories might include the following: Tithes and Contributions; Savings; Personal Expenses (lunches, haircuts, grooming, and school supplies); and Fun (activities, hobbies, books, and magazines).

☐ With an older child, additional finance skills can be practiced. Try some borrowing and lending within the family. Concepts such as promissory notes, interest, credit history and risk, collateral, and foreclosure can quickly become living realities.

☐ Let your child observe you when it's time to figure your taxes. Discuss the purpose of taxes and what public services they are used to provide. Explain the difference between income taxes, property taxes, luxury taxes, and sales taxes.

☐ Take your child for a visit to the bank. If you can, arrange for a brief tour. Have him or her come prepared with questions about banking and finance.

☐ When you think he or she is ready, open a checking account for your child. Your junior high or high schooler will soon realize that money doesn't grow on trees. And he or she will gain first-hand experience at distinguishing between wants and needs, and between price and value. Compliment the child's good choices, and when poor choices are made, help him or her understand why.

☐ If you can arrange it, let your son or daughter participate with you in a real investment such as a few shares of stock, a money fund, or even some real estate. This exposure can prepare the child for more insightful and mature money management in the future.

☐ Through it all, your example is crucial. A child will learn to save money, energy, and time, and to prioritize financial choices, as he or she sees you doing it. Invite your child to participate in understanding the choices you make, such as when you buy a tool or do a repair instead of calling a repairman. Let him or her observe as you pay the month's bills and balance the budget. Wisdom gained in this way can save major calamities later on.

If you do your job, the world of finance and economics with its pitfalls and opportunities will be no mystery to your child. He or she will become an adult knowing not only how to make a living, but how to live!

9

GIVING AND RECEIVING CRITICISM AT HOME

IT is a secure and mature person who can receive criticism and calmly evaluate it. Even wiser is the one who can give criticism in a constructive and winsome way. Wiser still is the parent who can develop these qualities in children.

Few other skills can better promote strength of character, healthy self-esteem, and stability throughout the storms and inequities of life. But even though the role of critic is an ancient and respected one, talking about criticism is tough. Too often criticism degenerates into condemnation. No wonder we're cautious about becoming critics. Just consider some of the warnings in Scripture.

"He who restrains his words has knowledge, and he who has a cool spirit is a man of understanding. Even a fool, when he keeps silent, is considered wise" (Prov. 17:27, 28, RSV). "Let every man be quick to hear, slow to speak, slow to anger, for the anger of man does not work the righteousness of God" (James 1:19, RSV). And perhaps the best known warning of all, spoken by Jesus himself: "Pass no judgment, and you will not be judged. For as you judge others, so you will yourself be judged, and whatsoever measure you deal out to others will be dealt back to you" (Matt. 7:1, NEB).

On the positive side, Scripture instructs us: "Like apples of gold in pictures of silver . . . is a wise reprover upon an obedient ear" (Prov. 25:11, 12, KJV). "Faithful are the wounds of a friend" (Prov. 27:6, KJV). "Therefore, putting away falsehood, let everyone speak the truth with his neighbor, for we are members one of another" (Eph. 4:25, RSV).

With these cautions and encouragements as a backdrop, let's consider some principles of healthy criticism:

- Criticize the action rather than the person.
- Don't criticize in anger. You'll usually overreact.
- Don't criticize when you're fatigued or under some other stress. Wait until your mind is clear and your mood is positive.
- Get all the facts—every situation has at least two sides.
- Give criticism in love, clearly and thoughtfully. Choose words that aren't emotionally charged. Absolutes like "always" and "never" hurt and usually exaggerate the truth.
- Don't criticize by comparing the person with someone else. In particular, don't compare siblings with each other, and *never* compare your spouse unfavorably with one of your parents.
- Often the things that irritate us the most in others are the faults we have ourselves. "Why do you see the speck that is in your brother's eye, but do not notice the log that is in your own eye?" (Matt. 7:3, RSV). Before you criticize a specific habit or trait, ask yourself if you have the same problem!

- Try to include a positive alternative to the negative action, attitude, or habit you're criticizing.

In receiving criticism, remember these insights:

- Receiving criticism is most difficult when we mistakenly feel that what we *do* is the same thing as what we *are*.
- Always consider the source when deciding how much weight should be given to a criticism.
- Give the person a chance to finish what he or she is saying before you attempt a response.
- The best immediate response to criticism is to attempt to clarify. Make a statement such as "What I hear you saying is. . . ." Don't react with self-defense.
- When the criticism is justified, thank the person and, if necessary, ask his or her forgiveness.

These principles for giving and receiving criticism can be applied by parent and child alike. Remember, though, that the examples we set as parents teach the most. The most profound lectures to our children aren't enough to mask a hypocritical life-style. Our children know us too well.

To help your children learn how to give and receive criticism, try these exercises:

☐ Participate with your child in a little self-criticism, being sensitive to how much your youngster's self-image can tolerate. Set the pace by confessing some way you fail as a parent. Invite your child's comments and reactions. Ask your child to identify one of his or her own failures. Make constructive suggestions to each other, pray together, and promise your mutual support in these specifics.

☐ Talk about the value of seeking out constructive criticism from others. Discuss some occasions when you've done this and how it helped. Seeking criticism from an objective, trusted friend is a great way to learn how to receive criticism. Help your child realize that seeking constructive criticism is not a sign of weakness, but of genuine strength.

☐ Help your child understand ways he or she can deal with the destructive criticism the child receives from peers and authority figures. One useful response is to acknowledge that the criticism has been heard without responding to it. This may sound something like, "I'm sorry you feel that I...." Another effective response is to assume for a moment that the speaker may have some truth in what he or she is saying and agree. Such a dialogue might go something like this:

"You did a terrible job!"

"Yes, I probably could have done that better."

"You certainly could have. That was awful!"

"Yes, it really looks bad, doesn't it?"

About this point, most critics begin to run out of things to say, and their tension is defused.

☐ Stage a family discussion about criticism and do some role playing. Talk first about the principles of criticism we've discussed, then make a game of giving and receiving critical comments. Use the response techniques mentioned above. Begin with simple situations, and watch for violations of the principles. Help the person rephrase his or her words. Practice like this can help form new patterns of response when it's no longer a game.

Most of all, remember to practice what you preach. How blessed is the parent or the child who has loyal critics and knows how to receive their help!

10

CAN YOUR CHILD HANDLE STRESS?

STRESS. Anyone alive in this shaky, competitive, fast-paced world of ours experiences a good deal of it, including our children. A child's life may seem carefree compared to that of a corporate executive—but children suffer from stress just as adults do. Only the symptoms are different.

A child's equivalent of the executive ulcer can be anything from frequent colds to reading problems. Behavior symptoms often involve withdrawal, a decrease in verbal expression, or unusually aggressive behavior. Physical responses might include diarrhea, itching, skin problems, a change in eating habits, or nightmares.

Beyond the immediate consequences of stress in children, we should keep in mind as well that studies show a high correlation between continuing stress into adulthood and health problems such as high blood pressure, heart disease, and cancer. For all these reasons, then, it is important that children develop good patterns for dealing with stress.

Stress is basically wear and tear on the body. Some stress is normal and necessary for healthful living. It keeps the mind agile and the circulatory system functioning. It also spurs us to do well on exams, to compete better in athletic events, to love and cry and strive for a more satisfying life.

But when stress becomes distress, the problems in health and behavior begin. The possible sources of unhealthy stress in children are many, including events such as a move to a new town, a chronic illness, the birth of a sibling, or the loss of a loved one. Stress may originate internally as a result of faulty relationships or destructive behavior. Or it may stem from some external and uncontrollable situation or event.

How can we help children lessen the sources of stress and cope with the stress that will still be inevitable? Much depends on whether we can pinpoint the source. If so, we can often deal with the problem directly. If, however, the reason for stress is hidden and diffused, sometimes the best we can do is help a child work out a strategy for coping with it.

How you handle stress as a parent will set an example for your child. Here are some approaches for both you and your child to consider:

☐ Talk about it. One of the worst responses to stress is to hold it in—to feel that you're alone in facing the problem. Create opportunities for a young child to express his or her emotions. Hand puppets and drawing are good activities in this regard.

☐ As a child grows older, he or she is more able to identify and analyze frustrations. Be sensitive to the child's comments that might be clues to anxiety. A mention of the school bully or the divorce of a friend's parents may be the time for some gentle questioning to bring hidden fears out into the open where they can be overcome.

☐ Visualize possible solutions together. Help your child identify specific actions he or she can take to resolve a stressful situation. If the problem, for example, is his or her falling behind in school, talk about how the child can better schedule time, improve study habits, use your help, or obtain more help from teachers. A little creative brainstorming can go a long way toward finding solutions. And often, because of worry, a simple solution has been overlooked.

☐ When an interpersonal relationship in your child's life is involved, help him or her assess where responsibility for the problem lies. The child may wrongly be taking responsibility for another's actions over which he or she has no control.

☐ Check out God's Word on a problem. One of the great privileges of Christians is that we can cast our cares upon the Lord, and receive genuine peace and rest in return (Rom. 8:26-28). Honest prayer can relieve stress. Pray with your child. Simple obedience may be the proper solution if he or she is violating one of God's principles for living.

☐ Live one day at a time. Most of the things both children and adults worry about never happen. A focus on the here and now can be healthy. Sometimes we just need to enjoy the present moment and postpone dealing with the source of stress until a more appropriate time. Suggest to your child that he or she not worry about a problem until you can talk about it together in a relaxed setting.

☐ Allow your child adequate time for play. It's one of the most important channels a child has for dealing with stress. Invest in toys that give the greatest scope to the child's imagination and creativity, such as clay, blocks, or woodcarving tools.

☐ Make sure everyone in your family gets adequate sleep and exercise.

☐ Limit the amount of TV your child watches. Too much TV watching results in stress from informational and emotional overload.

☐ Don't use your child as therapist. A single parent is especially tempted to unload problems on children because no other adult is in the home. Find a relative, close friend, or clergyman to listen instead.

☐ Avoid pushing your child into athletic, academic, or artistic competition, or setting unrealistic goals for achievement.

☐ Arrange if possible for each child to have his or her own private space—even if it is just the corner of a room—where he or she can go to be alone.

☐ Try to make some portion of the day a regular quiet time in your home, when radio, TV, and even the phone are unplugged.

☐ Share relaxing moments with your child. Stop to watch a sunset, examine a flower, admire a birdsong.

☐ Finally, laugh a lot together! The healing power of laughter has long been recognized as an effective antidote for stress.

No one, not even a child, can escape stressful situations altogether. But we can reduce to a manageable level the sources of wear and tear on our family members and help them control the effects of stress. The reward will be healthier, happier lives.

11

DEALING WITH DEATH

DEALING with death has never been easy, but in a culture that worships youthfulness, learning to cope with death is especially difficult. Mature models are scarce. And for children who are just beginning to learn about death, the loss of a pet, relative, or friend is a traumatic and bewildering experience.

The best way to help a child cope with bereavement will depend on several factors, including the child's age, the closeness to the child of the person who died, and the circumstances of death. Before you can help your child, however, you need to be aware of your own response to the event.

Grief is usually experienced in several stages, both by children and adults. In particular, we need to be aware that no matter how strong our faith in God, we're likely to experience stages of denial and anger that must be faced and overcome rather than repressed. Though we shouldn't hide these feelings from our children—they need to know that we feel them, too—we should depend on other adults to act as soundboards and to help us work out our acceptance of the event. A child should never be put in the role of counselor.

☐ A young child may ask questions about death when a pet or relative dies. These questions should be answered as honestly as possible, without either evasiveness or unnecessary details. A young child is apt to respond to the death of someone close by feeling guilty, because the child may remember being angry at the deceased and thus reason that the death is his or her fault. The child must be helped to realize that his feelings had no relationship to the event. He should also be helped to overcome feelings of rejection—that the loved one intentionally abandoned him.

☐ If the death took place as a result of illness or in a hospital, care should be taken not to allow the child to form a close association between death and sickness. Otherwise the child may experience deep fears whenever he or she is ill or in the hospital. Small children should not be told that death is a sleep from which the deceased will never awake. Many children who've been told this develop a fear of going to sleep at night.

☐ Whether or not a small child should go to a funeral is debated; children over five or six are better able to understand and handle the experience. During the period following a death, the child should remain in the home even though the parents are displaying grief. A child feels grief, and he or she needs to see others grieving as well.

☐ At about eight years of age, a child begins to understand the inevitability and irreversibility of death. At this point, he or she needs the freedom to bring up and discuss the subject. Avoid ridicule or shame and be sensitive to the child's fears.

Uncertainty, aggression, and shyness are often expressions of fear at this age.

☐ A good experience is to include your child in a memorial service. Prepare him or her by talking about each part of the service, and point out that its purpose is to allow family and friends to recognize the good things about a person's life. If there is an open-casket review, let the child choose whether he or she will look or touch.

☐ An adolescent is better able to understand the full implications of dying and the finality of death. In a period already full of emotional turmoil, a teenager needs room to express feelings freely without judgment. The young person may desire privacy to sort out his or her thoughts, and may turn to other adults or even peers for emotional support.

☐ At any age, your child needs to understand death as well as he or she can in the context of faith. The Bible teaches that death is universal (Ps. 89:48, Heb. 9:27), a result of sin (Rom. 6:23, James 1:15), and an enemy (Luke 22:39-44, Matt. 26:36-44, 1 Cor. 15:26). In facing death, Christians are to grieve, but not without hope (1 Thess. 4:13). By your example, encourage your child to acknowledge to God any feelings of anger, fear, or rejection. And soothe those feelings by remembering God's promises, his caring presence, and his unconditional love.

☐ Agree with your child that everything that happens in life does not always seem fair or consistent. A realistic attitude will relieve him or her of any guilt in feeling responsible for the loss.

☐ Cherish together the promises in Psalms 23:4 and 116:15. The unknown is a fearful thing, but believers are promised an escort (John 14:1-3) and a resurrection (1 Thess. 4:13-18, 1 Cor. 15:51, 52). We adults cannot fully understand death, but we can learn to trust God in the face of it.

Though God's presence in sorrow is immensely encouraging, it does not eliminate grief. We are still human. In your example of freely trusting and facing the uncertainties of life, your child will learn that it is OK to hurt, and that our true feelings can be acknowledged and expressed without shame. In helping your child learn to cope with death, you'll be setting him or her free to enjoy life.

12

WILL YOUR CHILD SUCCEED AT LOVE AND DATING?

WHAT are the odds that your son or daughter will succeed at marriage and family life? Not good when you consider our increasingly permissive moral climate, the failure rate of young marriages, and the power of peer pressure.

One of the biggest hurdles a parent faces is overcoming the prevailing notions about love and sex that permeate our culture through the media. The beliefs most often presented are that love at its best is a sentimental emotion coupled with passionate sexual feelings, and that sex is healthiest when given unrestrained expression.

Amid bankrupt ideas like these, it is not hard to see why our children often find heartbreaking trauma in dating, and their young marriages fail. The habits and patterns of relationships in dating are carried along into marriage. If love has been mostly a game, there's little hope it will be different after a wedding ceremony.

How, then, can you help your child as he or she discovers "love" and begins dating? Here are some guidelines:

☐ Morally responsible relationships in dating are deeply influenced by the strength of a child's self-esteem. Insecurity about his or her worth to God and a sense of self-importance will lead the young person to look for identity in a prematurely close relationship with a boyfriend or girl friend. The pull to express sexual feelings can be very strong. Since self-esteem is built largely by parents during early childhood, you can't begin too early to build toward success later.

☐ An equally vital principle is parental modeling. The patterns of relationship your child observes between you and your spouse will be accepted as the norm in male-female relationships. A healthy marriage is your best shot at overcoming the artificial and distorted models your teenager sees on TV and in the movies.

☐ It is important that you begin talking with your son or daughter about actions and values in love, sex, and dating before these topics become red-hot among his or her peers. Your child needs to sense that you know what's going on and can be a source of helpful answers to questions. Point out that the answers friends may offer are commonly rooted only in rumor, and may be completely false.

☐ Establish a set of objective criteria for preparation, which must precede your child's first date. This should include at least three areas:

☐ 1. Your child should first be able to demonstrate a pattern of responsibleness and mature decisions in other areas such as chores at home and school work. Let your child know that if he or she has not been responsible in these areas, dating will have to be preceded by some measurable changes.

☐ 2. Insist that your teenager locate, read, and become conversant with the key ideas in the Bible and other reliable literature about love, sex, and marriage. One especially good book is *Preparing for Adolescence* by Dr. James Dobson (Vision House). Then discuss the important issues together.

☐ 3. Have your teenager develop and write down his or her personal philosophy of love and dating. When you're satisfied with the document, endorse it with your signature. This paper should include a set of standards he or she is committed to maintaining about whom to date, where to go and where not to go on dates, curfews, and limits for expressing physical affection. Other important issues to tackle are going steady, dating non-Christians, and dating persons who are considerably older.

☐ Review practical tips for dating, such as the courtesies involved: how to ask for a date, meeting a date at the door, occasions that call for flowers, punctuality, and making reservations. Talk about the importance of meeting a date's parents and understanding their dating guidelines. And finally, of course, make sure your teenager knows what to do if the car breaks down or a more serious emergency occurs.

☐ As you talk over your child's written philosophy and standards, discuss the difference between external and internal controls—that is, the limits *you* can set on the young person's behavior as opposed to the *self-restraint* he or she must exercise. After all, the healthiness of his or her dating patterns will not depend ultimately on your rules, but rather on the choices your teenager makes when you're not around. So be sure to talk about the positive side of curfews and other boundaries you will establish.

☐ While an increasing quest for independence will characterize your child's adolescence and dating, you can encourage a continuing healthy tie to your family by making your home a magnet for his or her friends. Plan fun events, adopt a recreational hobby they can join you in, gain their respect, and learn to talk easily with them about serious topics. It'll cost you something in food bills and a loss of privacy, but your reward will be peace of mind and closeness with your teenager.

Your child can succeed at love and dating, but he or she will need your help and your consistent prayers. Your child's reward—and yours—will come as he or she builds a strong family and an enduring happiness.

13

YOUR CHILD CAN BE
NEAT AND CLEAN

REMEMBER the old proverb,
"Cleanliness is next to godliness"? If only our kids had that one
tattooed on their minds! The unbelievable messes they leave
behind them are convincing evidence that the value of neatness
is one that doesn't come naturally and must be learned. And
the only way they'll learn the value of cleanliness and orderliness is through consistent example and persistent instruction.

Fortunately, because cleanliness and orderliness are learned
traits, they can be acquired as positive habits that replace the

poor ones we may tend to have otherwise. But the big question is how?

- The answer lies first in your communication skills as a parent. Your goals for your child must be communicated effectively before he or she can attempt to fulfill them. And the primary objective your child must learn in this matter is to become a self-disciplined individual.
- A child needs to know that your basic desire is for him or her to become responsible for himself. If the child doesn't catch on to the goal of self-control, your efforts at reforming behavior will be constantly frustrated. But if the child does acquire a sense of self-responsibility, your work as a parent will decrease and the healthy habits will stay with him or her into adulthood.

Keeping in mind that much of your communication to your child is nonverbal—spoken through attitudes and actions—let's pinpoint some ways you can teach the value of cleanliness and neatness:

☐ Begin by asking two tough questions: (1) Is there any behavior I'm expecting of my child that I'm not consistently modeling myself? (Do I leave my things lying around? Do I clean up any messes I make? Am I sloppy according to my own standards?) (2) Is the level of orderliness I'm expecting appropriate to the developmental level of my child? (Expecting adult behavior from children almost always results in failure.)

☐ Make sure your child knows how to do the tasks you require of him or her. A child needs instruction in how to hang up clothes, straighten a room, or clean a bathtub. Try performing a chore together once to show how it's done. An excellent guide for children on how to approach cleaning up their own rooms (often a major and overwhelming undertaking) is Joy Wilt Berry's *What to Do When Your Mom or Dad Says, "Clean Your Room!"* (Living Skills Press, 1981).

☐ Avoid the sergeant syndrome. You know the stereotype of the tough sergeant barking orders at the helpless private.

The private complies only because he's afraid not to. But what he says about ol' sarge when he's back in the barracks is highly unflattering! The application to the parent-child relationship is obvious. You are far more effective as a parent when you can motivate your child with something more than fear.

☐ Replace orders and commands with choices. "Which would you rather do—clean up your room, or watch no TV tonight?" The ball is then in the child's court. If he or she chooses not to clean the room, the child is making a conscious decision to lose TV privileges. Giving him or her such a choice forces a decision-making process based on self-responsibility. And that's the best training of all!

☐ Combine gentleness with firmness, without anger. If anger often accompanies your firm requests, your child will learn not to respond until he or she senses the anger rising.

☐ When your requests are resisted, don't be surprised. It's normal. Calmly indicate that you mean what you say, and there is no use arguing. For example:

"Joan, I'd like you to clean the sink before your mother gets home."

"But Daddy, I want to go outside."

(Calmly) "I know you'd like to be outdoors with your friends, and you can go as soon as you clean the sink. The scouring pad's in the cabinet."

Note here that the parent didn't give in to the sergeant syndrome. He recognized the child's desires but remained firm with his request. Children will obey once they know that pleading won't do any good. At this point it's your patience that will keep things from getting unpleasant.

☐ Avoid evaluations. Your child is constantly under evaluation by authority figures. He or she is told to make good grades, be a good child, do a good job. Certainly there's no crime in being good, but when a child's prime motivation is to please the authority involved, the focus is on compliance rather than responsibility.

☐ Provide some flexibility in your requests. When possible, let the child fit your request into his or her own schedule—

provided, of course, the freedom isn't abused. And if it is, give choices: "Would you rather I choose the time when you take your bath, or will you choose for yourself?"

☐ Sidestep power struggles. Children have a tendency to argue when they feel it will help their cause. Without being cold-hearted, make sure argument never gets your child anywhere. This doesn't mean he or she has no part in the decision-making process. It does mean that when you know your instruction to a child is in his or her best interests, there's no need defending it to deaf ears.

In all your instructive efforts, let patience be your guide. Children will be children. They are not little adults. When your child feels your patient love behind your requests, he or she will respond more favorably, even if the child isn't yet convinced that cleanliness and orderliness are important. But the time will come when your child will learn to value these qualities and take a mature pride in possessing them.

PART TWO

ATTITUDES

Kids may forget what you said . . .
but they'll never forget
how you made them feel.
Carl W. Buehner

Your attitude should be the kind that
was shown us by Jesus Christ.
Philippians 2:5, TLB

14

YOU CAN SUCCEED AT TEACHING SUCCESS

PROBABLY not long ago you said to yourself, "I really don't care so much what Danny or Jennifer end up doing, I just want them to do their best and be successful at whatever they do."

Success is valued highly in our culture—you could even consider our society to be success-oriented. It's no wonder that our children daily feel the inescapable pressure to succeed. The pressure has many sources: parents, teacher, peers, even TV and magazines that hold up for imitation countless "successful" personalities in sports, entertainment, politics, and business.

Of all these sources, however, the one with the most influence is *you*. What you communicate about the importance of success will largely determine whether your child blossoms or buckles in the process of growing up "successfully."

- The key issue is helping the child define success. He or she needs a clear alternative to our world's definitions: money, popularity, power. We must encourage our children to see genuine success in life as the accomplishment of God's will—living lives that are satisfying to us because they are pleasing to him. We will succeed as parents if we can help our children discover a personal sense of worth and identity in being a "success" in God's eyes.

  Within that overall goal, we also must help our children achieve the small successes that are the building blocks of a fruitful life. As they build a successful pattern of accomplishing tasks, mastering skills, and acquiring character qualities, they'll gain the competence and confidence they need to tackle the great achievements that await them. Here are some important guiding principles:

- Distinguish carefully between your need to feel successful and your child's desires. ("But Dad, I don't even *want* to play football!")

- Increase your child's opportunities for success by cooperating with his temperament, abilities, and present limitations. (Given a short attention span, for example, two fifteen-minute music lessons may be better than one thirty-minute lesson.)

- Praise and punishment are useful, but encouragement is even better. Consistent encouragement builds up your child by focusing on his or her worth even when no particular accomplishment has taken place. ("You're a neat person to live with—I love you just for what you are, even when you're not doing anything special.")

- Encourage your child to relish and express the pleasurable feelings that accompany success (elation, fulfillment, satisfaction, confidence).

- Avoid using threat of failure to motivate your child. ("If you don't get good grades, you'll never amount to anything in life.") These threats often become self-fulfilling prophecies.
- Help your child experience success in his or her own unique ways. Cultivate the natural differences between brothers and sisters—don't expect one to follow in another's footsteps.
- Guide your child in selecting worthy goals. Help your son realize, for example, that dating standards are more important than taking out more girls than anyone else at school.

Meanwhile, remember that every child has an inborn urge to succeed. Only the very discouraged won't try to please parents, teachers, and God. And crippling discouragement can be avoided by helping children view themselves as valuable individuals created uniquely by a God who loves them.

☐ With a preschooler, your open display of delight over a new accomplishment does wonders for his or her emerging self-esteem. It's hard to give a preschooler too much physical affection. And succeeding at picking up toys is more fun when you offer a helping hand sometimes.

☐ An elementary-school child feels success especially when accepted as a valued peer-group member. School work and household chores take on greater meaning when they are important to the group. You can capitalize on this by planning ways for the child to help brothers, sisters, or friends accomplish tasks.

☐ For a preadolescent, individual and group achievement outside the family begin taking on special significance. Cooperate with this development and stay close to your child, especially as he or she begins to feel and understand his or her developing sexuality.

☐ A high school young person needs strong adult role models to reinforce positive growth and independence. Find ways to involve your teenager with you at work and at play. Go on a "date" with your teenager; take him or her on a business trip, arrange multiple family activities. Offer unlimited encouragement to help your child be a success on his or her first job.

Finally, let's face it. You must model the success values you teach. How have you defined success in your own life? And how have you achieved it? Draw your child close enough to you to identify with your own successes—and failures, too. Above all, remember that successful living is a process, not a product.

15

CHORES, CHILDREN, AND CHARACTER THEY GO TOGETHER!

THE chores we did as children are a fond memory for most of us. But sadly, many children today are missing the valuable character qualities regular chores build. Chores have become a lost development tool in our society's quest for leisure and labor-saving devices.

Even so, assigning chores is a most productive way of teaching responsibility and accountability to children. In our industrialized society, most children are no longer able to learn adult work skills by joining their parents on the job (such as working in the fields). Most adult activities are too technically complicated for children to help, and the workplace is far from home.

The home, however, can still be a place for learning skills that accomplish genuine work. The result is the development of valuable qualities such as diligence and perseverance, as well as a sense of satisfaction in the child. And as he or she begins to build competence, along with it will come self-confidence.

In addition, there are several educational benefits to teaching younger children domestic skills. Counting and arithmetic games, for example, can take place while washing dishes; sorting silverware helps them acquire sophisticated matching skills; and setting the table teaches right from left. In fact, almost all chores help a child learn to follow directions and carry out activities with several steps in sequence—an important foundation for many other educational skills.

Before an attempt is made to help your child develop character through chores, make sure you and your spouse are in agreement on these basics: (1) How you perceive the division of labor between male and female roles needs clear definition. (2) A high view of family democracy should underpin the plan you establish and enforce. (3) Recognize that while the child may not perform the work up to your standards at first, the main goal is his or her growth and improvement through the process. (4) Whatever strategy you have for assigning chores, it's bound to be frustrated eventually without regular and solid family communication.

Here are some basic principles to follow in developing your child's character through chores:

☐ Start early. Even a three-year-old can pick up toys, and then learn progressively other skills such as making beds and putting dirty clothes in the hamper or clean clothes in drawers. A five-year-old can set tables, dust, dry dishes, even vacuum (though you'll have to help with corners). A chore may take three times as long when the child does it, but he or she will take great delight in accomplishing "real grown-up work."

☐ Don't discourage volunteers. Between the ages of eight and twelve, children go through an especially helpful period when they want to model their parents.

☐ Whenever possible, cooperate with the interests and abilities of your child in assigning chores. Children take great pride in getting good at something they want to do.

☐ Divide and rotate the less desirable and the most popular tasks equally among all the family members.

☐ Spell out each task in writing and make clear the standard of performance for a job well done. Leaving this up to individual interpretation creates problems. At the same time, give tips for accomplishing each task better, faster, and more easily.

☐ Create and display a chart where assignments and performance are logged.

☐ Don't spare the praise. If you spend more time criticizing a poorly done job than praising a good one, you've actually rewarded the negative behavior more than the positive performance. Lavish compliments are fun to give and never hurt anyone.

☐ While opinions vary, most parents feel that no pay should be given for legitimate responsibilities that come with being a part of the family. Only extraordinary chores an outsider would normally be hired to perform deserve some pay. (An allowance is a better way to meet a child's regular need for some money.)

☐ Use chores to create and support a sense of family uniqueness and tradition. Adopt slogans such as "We cooperate to make things work for everyone," and "In our home rights and responsibilities are shared by all."

☐ If you're just starting a chores system, involve everyone in the planning. List the various tasks and problems that arise with each, and talk about why everyone needs to share the load. Remember that children carry out duties they have helped set for themselves much more readily than those that are imposed upon them. They should even help decide what the penalties are for chores neglected or poorly done.

☐ To improve consistency as you go along, a "when-then" policy is often helpful. When you see the desired performance (or something close to it), then reinforce it with praise, privileges, or experiences the child wants.

☐ From time to time help your child do the designated chores. He or she will see an attitude of servanthood in you worth imitating, and the work will provide a natural context for conversation and sharing.

Through it all, try very hard to be fair. It is the key to developing the mature sense of responsibility and accountability you want for your child. Chores—they can be both fun and rewarding!

16

DOES YOUR CHILD HAVE KAKORRHAPHIOPHOBIA?

HERE'S a question for you: Which is worse, the fear of failure, or failure itself? In reality, it's our fear of failure and bad feelings about failures that cripple us much more than the act of failing. Some people fear failure so much they develop a phobia about it—kakorrhaphiophobia! And it becomes a self-fulfilling prophecy.

This type of fear is prevalent in our society because we tend to worship success. It's particularly dangerous because it can isolate and paralyze us. The moment we begin any project, we risk failure, and one way to make sure we don't fail is simply to avoid attempting anything. We may become withdrawn and reluctant to venture into new realms of life. And if we're forced by circumstances to perform or compete, our fear may cause a host of psychological and physical reactions to the stress.

Most of us who must deal with a strong sense of failure are probably still trying to meet an impossible standard established in our own childhood—by a parent, perhaps, or even ourselves. We may still be attempting to earn the approval of someone whose opinion is important to us, and feeling as if we can't no matter how hard we try.

In the same way, the extent of our children's fear of failure will be determined to a great degree by our expectations and reactions to their attempts to succeed. If our kids experience frequent failures (in school, on a job, or in making friends), they can begin feeling as if they *are* a failure. They lose their sense of self-worth and think of themselves as "not good enough." The deepest, most destructive forms of guilt and hopelessness often follow, unless we intervene to make a difference.

As parents our task is to help our children see themselves as the beautiful creations of God they are, even though they fail. Here are some strategies for helping your child:

☐ Assess your child's strengths, aptitudes, and areas where growth is needed. Then gently guide him or her into activities where success will be most likely and unnecessary failures can be avoided.

☐ When your child does fail, help the child see what he or she did right, in spite of failure. Help the child assess the mistakes that were made and what could have been done differently. Stress the value of the effort put out in the first place. Gentle handling and teaching here can set the stage for future success.

☐ Help your child when he or she fails by accepting failure yourself—both yours and the child's!

☐ Don't stress your child's failures or use them as weapons when you are angry. Downplay his or her failures and bring attention to successes.

☐ Listen actively for indications that your child is feeling like a failure. Remind him or her that failing at some task does not mean that the individual is a failure. Show that you respect your child for who he or she is and not for the quality of performance.

☐ Instill within your child the knowledge that it's OK to fail, and that everyone fails sooner or later. Just like you, he or she needs the courage to be imperfect.

☐ Guard against expressing displeasure by pulling away, showing disgusted facial expressions, name-calling, being silent, or giving more attention to other children—all very effective ways of robbing a child's self-respect and sense of worth.

☐ Remember that an older child isn't necessarily more tolerant of failure than a younger child. (Much rebellion and acting-out during teenage years is evidence of an inability to handle failure.)

☐ Model a positive attitude toward failure in your own life. When you fail, don't hide it from your child; talk with him or her about it honestly, and explain that you plan to "bounce back" with a new determination to succeed.

☐ A child with a pattern of chronic failure is often trying to fail. The individual feels so discouraged that he or she has given up hope of ever feeling worthwhile and lovable. Having despaired of trying to get attention, the child has lost the hope of being important enough to hurt his parents' feelings. Such a child is simply trying to prove his or her inadequacy in order to be left alone.

Obviously, such a child is emotionally damaged, and traditional disciplinary measures will only worsen the behavior. He or she needs vast amounts of encouragement, and probably professional help as well.

One last thing to remember: How do you feel when you fail at helping your child handle his or her failure? Don't catch kakorrhaphiophobia. Instead keep in mind the insights above, and look to God to help you succeed.

17
THE ENORMOUS GIFT OF SELF-ESTEEM

WE see and hear the term "self-esteem" frequently. Troublesome behavior in children, even neurotic behavior in adults, we're told, stems from a lack of feelings of self-esteem. But what exactly is it? What does self-esteem accomplish? And where do these feelings originate, especially in children?

Put simply, feelings of self-worth are internal thoughts and beliefs. They tell you that you're a worthwhile person, and that you're reasonably competent and likeable. When you choose to believe these ideas about yourself, you then expect others to see you this way and to like you. And because you're convinced that you're worthwhile, competent, and likeable, you'll tend to be open, friendly, optimistic, industrious, well-groomed, and venturesome.

On the other hand, if you or your child lack these feelings of self-esteem, and feel instead that you're rather incompetent, unlikeable, or unworthy, you'll tend to expect your efforts to fail. You'll anticipate that others will reject and abandon you, and expect your life to be a failure.

As a result, your energy will become focused on keeping others from discovering what you're really like. Because you expect rejection and criticism, you'll tend to be hostile, closed, and unfriendly. Expecting to fail, you'll become lazy, constricted, or erratic. And because you feel worthless, you'll neglect your health and appearance. Or you'll spend hours constructing a beautiful facade to fool everyone into believing you're a beautiful person.

When you understand this cause-and-effect relationship, its not hard to see how your responses to your child become his or her primary source of self-esteem. And self-esteem is fundamentally established through the experiences of childhood. The patterns of thought begun there are very difficult to change later on.

Self-esteem has three fundamental building blocks:

1. *The security of belonging.* This comes from experiencing a solid position of significance in the family.
2. *The satisfaction of achievement.* Each child needs a chance to be successful at something.
3. *The joy of feeling valued.* A child's happy awareness that he

or she is valuable is maintained through consistent, sincere praise.

Here, then, are some of the kinds of parental responses that will build healthy and positive feelings of self-esteem in your child. How do these compare with your present approach?

☑ First, take stock of your own reservoir of self-esteem. Parents need a positive self-image themselves in order to build one in their children.

☑ Provide a young child with opportunities to develop competence and confidence. Invest in toys, games, and crafts that enable the child to create and to succeed in mastering self and his or her environment.

Lance picks things too hard

example

☐ Allow your child to choose his or her own areas for achievement. Don't try to impose on your child the ambitions you had as a young person, or make him or her achieve what you didn't in sports, academics, or the arts.

☑ Genuinely listen to your child. It teaches the individual that he or she is an interesting person.

☑ Ask for your child's opinion about what to do in various problem situations. This will help the child discover that his or her judgment can be sound.

☑ If you raise questions (without ridicule) about your child's plans, you'll help the child find that he or she can be flexible and can reevaluate situations when new information is presented.

☑ See each child as an individual. Avoid comparing your children to each other. Emphasize unique strengths and weaknesses.

☑ Discuss your child—especially his or her problems—only when the child is not present.

☑ Be aware of your child's nicknames, especially those you use. Refrain from calling him or her by derogatory names, or even seemingly innocent labels such as "Turtle" that might suggest undesirable qualities. Develop positive names such as "Champ" or "Little Lady."

☐ When a child is kind, unselfish, neat, helpful, self-disciplined, creative, well-coordinated, industrious, or anything else that's praiseworthy, say so! Your child will learn that he or she can be successful in these ways. Sincere praise never hurt anyone!

☑ Point out and applaud your child's improvements, no matter how small. He or she will learn to be optimistic.

The opposite approach will obviously destroy self-esteem. Giving in to the tendency to be negative and condemning is the most effective way to make a child lose any sense of worth.

☐ Avoid condemning criticism and ridicule. They teach a child that something is basically wrong with him or her.

☐ Avoid constantly making decisions for your child. If you do, the child will conclude that his or her judgment is poor.

☐ Avoid pointing out your child's many failures and imperfections. It can only cause the child to lose any confidence in being competent. Soon the child will cease to like him or herself, and won't expect to be liked by anyone else, either. After all, "Dad and Mom are bigger, stronger, and smarter than I am, so their judgment must be right. There's something wrong with me!"

Based on the self-evaluation above, what is your child concluding about him or herself? What your child decides is terribly important. And only you can give the enormous gift of true self-esteem.

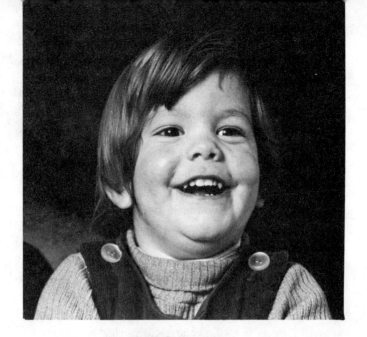

18

YOU CAN GIVE YOUR CHILD A THANKFUL SPIRIT

You know the feeling: with face beaming and eyes sparkling, your little "angel" comes bounding in from her first thrilling ride on the new swing set you bought her. "Oh, thank you, Mommy!" she squeals as her small arms squeeze around your neck. Or that feeling when your teenage son slaps you on the back and says, "Thanks, Dad, for letting me use the car. You're really OK."

You also know the embarrassment you feel when profound silence follows a gift your child has just received. Or your deep disappointment when a favor you've just performed goes completely unacknowledged.

What went wrong? What does it take to build a consistent and spontaneous spirit of genuine thankfulness in our children?

- Much recent research has indicated that nothing influences children's value systems more than the relationship they observe between their mom and dad. So how often and how openly does your child see you and your spouse expressing your appreciation to each other?

- Another key to stimulating a thankful spirit is your frequent expression of your appreciation for who your child is and what he or she does. In doing so you're affirming the child's self-esteem—and as the child feels more secure in your appreciation and approval, he or she will express personal thankfulness to others more freely.

But we still must wonder why this matter of thankfulness is so tough for kids. In the first place, when a child sincerely says thank you, he or she feels open and vulnerable, because it's an expression of dependence. That's why it's so important that we don't drown that small thankful spirit by demanding adultlike expressions of gratitude. We should be sensitive enough to require only that each child act his age in the way thanks is expressed.

It's also important to recognize that true thankfulness cannot be demanded. Making your child feel guilty for not feeling thankful doesn't accomplish much. A better approach is to look for the underlying message in his or her unthankful spirit. What do you hear? Insecurity, fear, anger, revenge seeking, or a desperate reach for attention might be what your child is giving vent to. And if you can hear the message and meet the need, a thankful spirit will soon be restored. The child will appreciate you for that kind of unconditional love.

There are some specific things you can do to build thankfulness in children of various ages. Here are a few:

☑ A preschooler is naturally very self-centered. It's a necessary part of healthy development. Most thanking at this age is done to gain approval for being good. Give your approval freely, and openly thank your child and God for the child's specialness.

☑ Try playing with your little one the "Thank You, Body" game. Take turns thanking your body parts for their respective functions, such as "Thank you, hands, for helping me eat."

☑ An elementary-age child responds well to making creative expressions of thankfulness. Help your child express gratitude to other family members by writing simple songs or poems, especially on occasions such as birthdays, Mother's and Father's Day, Valentine's Day, and anniversaries.

☑ Make a family tradition of giving homemade thank-you cards. People are constantly doing little things for us that we take for granted. Take a few minutes from time to time to create together a simple card or note for these small favors.

☑ As a family, play "Spin the Thank-You Bottle." The one who spins it must express a specific thank-you thought to the person the bottle points to. Then that individual spins it the next time. Talk about how good it feels to hear someone say thanks.

☑ Every once in a while, have the family compose together a thank-you letter to someone who has been a help to you: a grandparent, perhaps, or a baby-sitter or teacher. Think how the mail carrier would feel to find a thank-you note and a bag of cookies in the mailbox especially for him or her!

☑ The next time you have a few minutes to spare while riding in the car, try being thankful "from A to Z." Take turns thinking of things to be grateful for that begin with *A*, and thank the Lord for them: "Thank you, Lord, for apples … angels … alligators … automobiles." Then go on to *B*, *C*, and the other letters of the alphabet. Be flexible with hard letters like *X*. Use items like "X-cellent health" and "X-tra special friends."

☑ With a preadolescent, gift-giving and helping projects are particularly important expressions of thankfulness. At this age, a child has a greater ability to respond to other people's needs. And when in return the child's own needs are met, he or she will readily identify with the pleasure of saying thank you.

☑ Adolescence is another time of strong self-centeredness. The young person is beginning to see himself even more as an individual who is different from others. Make sure you're giving emotional as well as material gifts to your teenager—gifts such as respect, trust, and personal time.

☐ As a family, make it a habit to express your thanks to God openly and spontaneously. Make sure your family prayers begin with praise and thanksgiving before you make requests. Experience the joy of small things together with your child, such as the glory of the night sky or the happiness of a new puppy. Make the pleasure of these little occasions complete with an unashamed, out-loud "Thank you, Lord!" or even a song of thanks. And don't forget that even when things aren't going well, "Give thanks in all circumstances" (1 Thess. 5:18, NIV).

☑ Take the Thanksgiving holiday as a golden opportunity to focus on thankfulness in your family. Around the dinner table, have family members join in short expressions of thanks for specific gifts from God. During the meal, express thanks to each other.

Through it all, let each child see and hear your thankfulness for him or her. And thank *you* for being committed to effective parenting!

19
WHAT MAKES KIDS CREATIVE?

EVERY child is creative—about the mischief he or she gets into, if nothing else. But as children grow older, something seems to happen. That free-wheeling, often-admired spontaneity fades, and only a few people are able to continue living creatively in this era of mass production, depersonalizing bureaucracy, standardized forms, and electronic communication.

Nevertheless, we are made in the image of a Creator God, and his Spirit is in us to help us become creative in all we do. And though the degree of creativity in each of us is probably in part an inherited quality, there is much we as parents can do to cultivate the creative gifts in our children.

Above all, it's best to realize that creativity develops in a climate of respect where each child can gain a genuine sense of self-worth. Consistent love and praise and lots of hugs are the context in which creative spirit thrives. So let's look at some key principles and activities:

- Show confidence in your child's abilities; avoid the adult tendency to provide too many answers too quickly.
- Allow your child to take some risks. It will free you both to enjoy and explore your relationship. Creative freedom is a balance between responsible rule-keeping and a corresponding sense of adventure into the unknown.
- Regularly help your child experiment with new tools and materials. Avoid insisting that every action or result have a profound use. Genuine creativity often follows numerous failures.
- Encourage a young child to express him or herself in role play. It's OK for little boys to play with dolls, and little girls with trucks, if the child's parents are simultaneously modeling good male and female roles. Allowing your son the freedom to be sensitive and emotional, and your daughter the opportunity to be assertive and show initiative forms a healthy climate for creative expression.
- Stimulate your child through regular exposure to good books, music, and art. Rummage together through the public library, discover new stations on the radio, and visit the museums and art shops in your area. Creativity thrives on lots of exposure, because most creative acts involve putting parts of existing thoughts or objects together into new combinations. So the greater the exposure to new ideas and objects, the greater the potential for creative thinking.

☐ Avoid prejudicing too quickly your child's impractical notions with the dismissal "It won't work."

☐ Encourage questions. Though your preschooler may ask more questions than you care to answer, remember that a questioning mind is a creative mind. Help your child learn to ask better or more penetrating questions. Then search out the answers together.

☐ Develop a positive approach to the errors your child makes. While serious mistakes will require appropriate discipline, be sure to punish the behavior and not the person. Don't accompany correction with insults that attack your child's self-esteem, such as "That was a stupid thing to do!" or "You never do anything right!"

☐ Value your child's creations, performances, and experiments. Nothing more quickly kills a creative spirit than a hasty "Why'd you do that?" or "Leave that yucky mud alone." Post your child's art in prominent places and give compliments on his or her work in front of friends.

☐ Encourage make-believe. Puppet shows, homemade costumes, recitals, and impromptu dramas draw out the best in creative instincts and ideas. As with any other trait, a kid gets better at what he or she practices.

☑ Practice being a creative observer with your child. Take time to watch birds, weather, people, flowers, and animals. Notice processes as well as objects.

☑ Join your teenagers or lead your junior in writing a poem, keeping a journal, drawing illustrations, or building with your hands. Don't fret over the quality of the creation. Just lead enthusiastically!

☐ Select toys and activities that involve personal initiative. A balsa wood plane model, for example, may be a better choice than one with parts that snap together. Harmonicas, magnifying glasses, magnets, and cardboard boxes prompt much more creativity than most ready-made toys.

☐ Encourage your child to collect things: feathers, buttons, seeds, stamps, or anything else of special interest. Collecting stimulates an inquisitive and creative mind.

☑ Keep a selection of creative materials handy for your child's experimentation. Fun with clay, chalk, paints, paper, markers, glue, tape, old magazines, small cans and tubes, yarn, and pipe cleaners should be a part of every child's memories. Later, add dress-up clothes, hammers and nails, a camera and other media.

☐ Allow your older child to decorate his or her own room, creating an atmosphere that complements personal activities and joys.

☐ Encourage your child's verbal abilities through word games, rhyme making, and original stories, riddles, lyrics, and poems. Allow him or her to be present when adults are conversing; it's a good vocabulary stretcher. Read newspaper and magazine articles together and talk about them. Encourage letter writing.

True creativity involves independence, sensitivity, and flexibility. Like most values and character traits, these are initially molded by you. With only a little care and planning you can give your child the life-long gift of creativity.

For a closer look at this subject, see *Growing Creative Children* by Marlene D. LeFever (Tyndale, 1981).

20
GIVE YOUR CHILD A "CAN DO" SPIRIT!

If you've ever watched two-year-olds operate, you know the strength of their head-on, no-holds-barred, "I'm gonna do this, no matter what" spirit. It's marvelous!

In the ensuing years, that "can do" attitude becomes modified by many discouraging experiences, but psychologists tell us that negative feedback from others destroys our self-confidence the most. That puts the burden squarely on parents, because we can do much to help our children develop a successful "can do" spirit.

☐ Studies in human development show that people who have strong confidence in themselves tend to come from confident parents. So first of all, to build a confident attitude in your child, you need to have a confident response to the challenges in your own life. When you have a problem to solve, a challenge to meet, or a task to be done, look at it with assurance that you'll succeed. Your kid is watching.

☐ The next example you must set is your own confidence in your child. There are two primary ways to express it: state it verbally often, and trust the child with a job to do.

In his book *You Can Become the Person You Want to Be* (Revell, 1976), Robert Schuller lists these qualities of a self-confident winner: imagination, commitment, affirmation, and "never give up." Together the initials of these words spell "I CAN" (for easy remembering). Let's examine each of them more closely for ways to help your child build a successful attitude.

☑ *Imagination* involves both assessing a child's strengths and needs as well as letting him or her know that others also dream dreams and feel inadequate. You can help your child perceive his or her strengths as well as use imagination in a beneficial way. Take your child out for breakfast and let him or her know that you dream and fear failure, too. Talk together about the child's strengths and how to overcome his or her weaknesses.

☐ During family times, have family members share strong and weak points they see in each other, and close with some affirming prayer together. Be sure that temporary weaknesses such as physical development or age limitations are distinguished from more permanent ones.

☐ One purpose of imagination is to help your child visualize him or herself as the person he or she wants to become. It's also helpful for your child to hear about your past feelings of awkwardness, the school subjects you had trouble with, and your other failings. Knowing that you overcame them will help your child develop a forward-looking sense of expectancy for him or herself.

☐ Another part of imagination is our vision of who we are already—our self-image. Help your child shape this image by training him or her to *think* confidently. Teach the child

96

to identify and reject recurring thoughts such as "I just can't do it; I never do anything right," and to replace them with positive mental statements: "Of course I can—I did a good job last time!"

☐ *Commitment* to reaching visualized goals is the next essential in achieving success. Do you know your child's goals and dreams? Have you helped him or her evaluate them or plan for them? While this is easier for an older child, a young one has goals, too, such as learning to ride a bike, planning to own a pet, or preparing to build a tree house. At the same time, reveal to each child some of your own goals and ambitions. Commitment will involve not only the intensity of the child's desires, but also your supportive actions through personal help, encouragement, and resources.

☐ *Affirmation*, the next key, comes through successes. In the early stages, set your child up for successful experiences. Let him or her help you work on the car or cook a special meal. Ask your child to teach you something he or she knows that you don't. And avoid any hint that the ideas or activities are somehow "beneath" you.

Keep in mind that kids can often perform "grown-up" work better than we think. They can paint, help tune up the car, sort files at the office, check math on tax forms, or even keep track of the family budget. So think again about the helping activities you normally rule out for them.

☐ One key to assure success in your child's efforts is to make sure he or she is adequately trained and prepared for the tasks being attempted. Give the instructions and example necessary before your child begins to bake a cake, build a stock car, or try out for a sport. But don't overinstruct, especially with an older child who needs to figure out a few things on his or her own.

☐ At the same time, help your child aim for excellence. The child may not always achieve it, and when he or she doesn't, you should still be supportive. But consistently mediocre work will not be satisfying to a child, and will dull his or her self-confidence.

☐ *"Never give up"* is a quality shaped by patience and persistence. When your child seems to be failing at a task or falling short of a goal, be alert to encourage him or her to hang in there. Remind the individual of his or her past successes where persistence paid off. Offer your help, but only when it's obvious the child will quit and fail if you don't assist. And when you do help, don't take over. Add just enough assistance to assure success when combined with the child's continued efforts.

Finally, here are a few pitfalls to avoid:

- Don't keep a child from attempting new tasks, even if you're not sure of his or her success. If your son wants to make breakfast for the first time, let him try it—and give a few tips to help.
- Don't suggest failure by hovering over the child or saying something like, "You made a mess the last time you tried."
- Avoid excessive criticism, not only of your child, but of his or her friends. Refrain from comparisons with other children.

Henry Ford is credited with saying, "Think you can; think you can't; either way you're right." Your child's confidence that he or she *can* begins with you. If you believe your child can accomplish good things, chances are he or she will agree. Remember the principles of "I CAN." Apply them together—and you'll both be rewarded with success!

21

AWAKENING THE SERVANT IN YOUR CHILD

WHEN you dream of the "ideal" child, servanthood probably isn't the first character quality that comes to mind. Maybe that's a reason many in the "Me Generation" seem to be less concerned about being a servant than being served.

At the heart of the matter, a sensitivity to servanthood—even an instinct for it—is fundamental to balanced success in almost any of life's endeavors. Leadership suffers without it. The servant-leader who Jesus described—"whoever wants to become great among you must be your servant," Mark 10:43, NIV—is a better motivator and far more likeable than the one who leads through fear. A marriage without serving neither fulfills the partners nor lasts very long. And a human personality is in trouble when it doesn't gain a sense of fulfillment from serving the side of truth in moral issues, or from doing good to others.

So how does an instinct for servanthood become a part of your developing child? As in other areas, a child will learn best what he sees modeled most at home. Measure yourself with questions like these:

- In the course of daily living, does my child see me serving and helping willingly, even when I'm not being paid by my employer or nagged by my spouse?
- Does my child see me volunteering for extra chores at home when my spouse is pushed or bushed?
- Do I ever take the most menial chores around the household, or do I always assign the most unpleasant tasks to my child?
- Am I in the habit of looking for little ways to make life easier for my child, or do I think that's what he or she is supposed to be doing for me?
- Have I ever volunteered to do my child's chores when he or she was behind in homework and needed some extra time?
- Does my child see me frequently helping friends and neighbors, or serving as a volunteer in the community?

If all this sounds more like a lesson for parents than for kids, you're getting the message. The process starts with us. Then, in addition to our example, we can take some other steps to help our children learn the sacrifices that come with being a servant.

☐ Even a toddler can learn to be a "helper" to Mom and Dad. If you're willing to spend more time on a chore or project than it would take if you were working alone, you can give a little one the pleasure of "helping" you rinse the dishes, wash the car, pick up toys, or dust the furniture. If the child is reluctant, don't push the matter at this age; but it's most likely he or she will be anxious to be involved in what you're doing. Express your praise and gratitude for the service, and tell other family members frequently what a helper the youngster is. You may even find at times that a task is finished faster this way because the child isn't competing for your attention.

☐ When a child has reached four or five years of age and his or her sense of autonomy and identity is secure, begin involving the child in genuine help, such as pitching in on siblings' chores or assisting parents with a "blitz-cleaning" of the house just before guests arrive. Continue the praise and recognition for such service.

☐ Encourage your primary-school youngster to volunteer occasionally for service chores in the classroom, or to take a less glamorous chore intentionally for the pure sake of serving. This helps to counterbalance the emphasis on competition that permeates most schools and discredits the worth of service.

☐ Involve your child in a scouting program. Here peer pressure reinforces the value of service. This pattern of thinking and action can take root and mold character for a lifetime.

☐ With your older elementary-school child, talk about the role of servanthood and unselfishness in building friendships. Think with him or her about an act of service for a friend. Ask for a report on the friend's response. If it didn't go well, troubleshoot the reason and suggest a second try.

☐ With your preteen or teenager, study biblical texts about servanthood to understand what it means to say, "The first shall be last and the last shall be first," and "having this mind in us which was also in Christ Jesus." Here are some verses to discuss: Matt. 20:26-28; Mark 9:35; John 13:12-15; Romans 15:1-3; Gal. 6:10; and Phil. 2:3-8.

☐ Take photos of your child performing service tasks. Make sure these are praised each time you open the family scrapbook or show family slides.

☐ Ask the family to identify some group service projects that can be undertaken together—perhaps yard work for an elderly neighbor, correspondence with a lonely person away at school or in the service, or sponsorship of a refugee family. Or contact your local volunteer action center to find out which organizations could use some help.

Every month, take stock of your child's "servant quotient" as well as your own. Make sure serving is a frequent dinnertime conversation topic. Make your child aware that the mature person who is secure enough to serve is sure to become a leader in the best sense of the word.

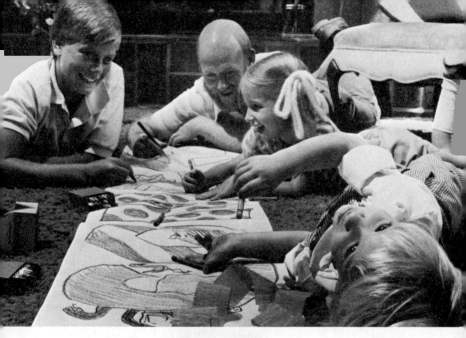

22

WITH YOUR KIDS, LAUGHING MATTERS

HUMORIST Craig Wilson is not just a funny man—he's actively involved in serious matters of life and faith. "Humor was as much a part of my growing up as was the Lord," he reflects. "Somehow it became clear to me that since God enjoys us, we are free to really enjoy ourselves as well. Whether it was role-playing each other's petty arguments or just dinnertime storytelling, in my home there was a constant drone of laughter."

What about your house? Is a good sense of humor and love of laughter one of the essential skills and attitudes your children will learn from you? Few attributes are better at promoting good health. In fact, as the book of Proverbs said long ago, "A cheerful heart is good medicine" (17:22, NIV). Laughter stimulates circulation, stabilizes blood pressure, oxygenates the blood, facilitates digestion, and massages the vital organs. It has even been shown to help the body deal with chronic pain.

Laughter is great spiritual medicine as well. It promotes a love for life, reduces stress, and smooths interpersonal relationships. Whether you consider yourself a "funny man" or not, you can employ a ready smile and a sense of wit to great advantage in your family.

- A sense of humor helps conscientious parents "allow kids to be kids." Strong expectations for behavioral perfection in childhood years can cause insecurity and a poor self-image in children. But when a good sense of humor is injected into correction, a concerned parent can bring about the desired behavior change in an atmosphere of gentle kidding rather than under the threat of punishment. Against this relational backdrop, moments of serious offense can be handled with appropriate intensity without damaging the basic grace that should exist between parent and child.

- Laughter can be cleansing to the human spirit, especially in moments of extreme crisis and emotion. Craig Wilson recounts that three days after his father was expected to die of cerebral malaria, Craig called the hospital to check on his progress. When the phone was answered in his father's hospital room, he heard a voice say, "Joe Hozenfeffer here!" Of course, that wasn't his dad's name—it was rather his favorite moniker, adopted long ago and used when calling a friend on important business or making a reservation at a restaurant. Craig's father had chosen that moment and that name to report jokingly that the worst was over.

- Nothing dispels tension and brings a sense of balance amid conflict like a round of laughter. Confrontation can be defused and tempers soothed with a bit of wit. Craig recalls one morning when his grandpa came down to breakfast with a soiled necktie. "What have you got that on for?" barked Grandma, pointing to the spot.

"What's wrong with it?" was his confused and innocent response.

"It's dirty!" she said.

"Well," he replied, looking around the room, "I guess that's a pretty serious charge against me!"

Everyone screamed with laughter, and to this day around the Wilson household, silly domestic skirmishes are often interrupted by someone mimicking, "That's a pretty serious charge against me!"

Here are some ways to promote laughter and a good sense of humor in your home:

☐ What you model is terribly important. So laugh at yourself and your own mistakes. Don't take yourself too seriously. The new perspective laughter gives you can help you see that a seemingly grave situation or burdensome problem is not really as tragic or insurmountable as you thought.

☐ In those dull moments when everyone's tired or the weather's lousy, laugh some together. Find some funny stories to read aloud, or go through a book of world records for such chucklers as the world's longest fingernails (usually there's a picture of the winner).

☐ Lighten up tedious or dull family chores with some good jokes or riddles. Make such regular drudgeries as dish washing or yard raking a designated time for sharing funny stories and jokes.

☐ Keep a young spirit through healthy practical joking. When family members think enough of each other to go out of their way to play good clean pranks, it says a lot about their mutual love and appreciation.

☐ Keep an eye out for spontaneously funny family moments that can be recorded and cherished in years to come. You may even find a standard "line" such as Craig Wilson's grandpa's remark that can be used again and again to break tension or elicit chuckles.

☐ With a toddler, tickle and laugh a lot. When you have to say no, say it firmly and follow it soon after with a smile. Humor injected into those minor moments of behavioral correction does wonders with a preschooler.

☐ Be careful to distinguish between healthy laughter and ridicule, sarcasm, or excessive teasing. Laughter heals. The others can wound.

☐ Clip cartoons to share with other family members or tape to the refrigerator or family bulletin board.

☐ Collect funny stories or incidents throughout the day and make it a habit to tell them at dinnertime. Spice up the meal with jokes and funny riddles as well. Laughter aids digestion!

☐ On family outings, make a point of noticing funny signs along the way, and listen to the foolish things people say in public. Recount those episodes later and embellish the details. Storytelling in this fashion sharpens everyone's powers of observation and attention to the details in life around us.

A childhood without laughter would be a dismal story indeed. Laughter is good medicine—and you can be the family doctor!

23

HELP YOUR CHILD KICK THE BLUES!

GROWING up is hard. It's painful. Kids don't become adults without considerable stress, and unpleasant emotions are a part of daily living for adults and children alike. At times, everyone feels down, discouraged, despondent, or bored. So learning to cope with these moments—even to value them—is one skill our children must acquire.

Kids (like adults) vary widely in their ability to kick the blues. Some can look at their feelings objectively and choose a different course. Others seem only able to justify their "right" to feel sad. It's a matter of both maturity and temperament.

As you help your child work through depression, consider these principles:

- Negative emotions are OK to express. They're normal, even rational and healthy responses to life's difficulties. Avoid giving the impression that feeling down is wrong.
- What we do with negative emotions involves our free choice and act of our wills. While we cannot always control our circumstances, we can control our responses to them by deciding to rise above situations and moods. Often we try to meet a legitimate emotional need, such as attention from others, with a poor method like pouting. But God desires to help us choose more constructive ways to meet the need.

Severe circumstances or a regular pattern of ineffective responses to depression may cause your child to feel unable to choose a more positive response. One or more of these symptoms might appear:

☐ 1. Lasting periods of moodiness, apathy, and unhappiness
☐ 2. Withdrawal from others
☐ 3. Disturbed sleep patterns
☐ 4. Change in eating patterns
☐ 5. Physical symptoms like indigestion, headaches, rashes, and pains
☐ 6. Decreased academic achievement
☐ 7. Aggressive or destructive behavior
☐ 8. Anxiety, nervousness, and agitation.

If any of these symptoms persist, seek professional help.

Normally, however, the following strategies can help your child win over unpleasant feelings.

☐ First let the child know you recognize the feeling. Then, if the apparent cause of the mood is relatively minor, divert attention to another interest or activity. This will often be the case when the child is preschool age. After a brief discussion, say, "Let's go do this" or "How about helping me?"
☐ If the cause of sadness is a deep one you share, such as the loss of a loved one, don't hide your own emotions. If you

feel like it, go ahead and join your child in the tears. The bond created by your willingness to reveal your own sadness will help you rise above the mood together.

☐ Feeling blue is often related to feeling lonely. Try giving your child more physical contact or time. Do it right then or plan a time when you can be together later in the day. Inviting a friend over or planning a future outing are also ways of breaking the "spell" of depression.

☐ Depression is sometimes the symptom of unresolved guilt. If the child is unable to pinpoint the source of sadness, gently explore together his or her recent behavior. Take an indirect approach, asking questions without making accusations. You may discover a hidden wrong that needs to be confessed and forgiven.

☐ Assist your child in the choice to overcome the mood. Exhortations to stop acting or feeling the way he or she does only reveal your distance and unwillingness to empathize. A better approach is to help your child verbalize the options: "You can either sit here and feel blue, or phone a friend, or play a favorite record, or do your chores so that you can play later, or...."

Keep emphasizing choice and counter any protests your child makes about the options by asking him or her to select better ones. Often a quick snack can get your child moving toward an effective decision.

☐ Encourage your child by communicating your belief in his or her strengths and abilities. Reminisce about past successes and times the blues were vanquished. Recall how the passing of a little time changes our perspective.

☐ Avoid being overly sympathetic. Too much sympathy suggests that your child is helpless. A better way to empathize is to recall a moment when you felt the way your child does now, and how you overcame it. Your identification with the problem affirms that the blues are normal and can be licked.

☐ Make sure your child is getting sufficient exercise. Certain chemicals released in the brain during physical activity naturally ward off depression.

☐ Remain sensitive. Time is on your side. You can't push a

child out of the doldrums. He or she has to come on his or her own. Your part is to remain tactfully available.

Above all, remember that your efforts are doomed unless your responses to your own moods model the godly perspective that "we also rejoice in our sufferings, because we know that suffering produces perseverance; perseverance, character; and character, hope" (Rom. 5:3-4, NIV). As one sign put it, "No Pain, No Gain." Your child can overcome unhappy emotions if you take the time to give him the tools.

24
TEACHING KIDS TO
FOLLOW THROUGH

C HILDREN play games "to the finish." So why do they find it hard to follow through with day-to-day tasks—a key to successful living? And how can parents help them gain this positive habit?

One hurdle to be overcome is that sticking with a task or skill until it's mastered isn't very popular today. We have a cultural bias toward the "instant fix" in foods, appliances, personal wants—even spirituality. Add to this the prevailing notion that society owes us a living, and it's obvious why kids aren't committed to perseverance.

How can you help your child learn to follow through? Keep in mind these motivational principles:

☐ To a preschooler, balance is important. At this age, your child is motivated primarily by rewards or punishments and can't understand that a job must be completed because it's the "right" thing to do. When the child is failing to finish an assignment, it's best to pitch in and help. This modeling communicates your support and the importance you attach to finishing the task. It also avoids the discouragement and tension nagging brings.

☐ Being sensitive to your youngster is critical. Low expectations won't challenge your child to reach his or her potential. Expectations set too high generate a devastating fear of failure. One way to emphasize the right principle is to read popular children's stories that reinforce the value of persistence, like *The Little Engine That Could*. Older children would enjoy reading the biographies of famous persistent people, such as Thomas A. Edison (who had to persevere in developing such inventions as the light bulb) or Martin Luther King (who persevered in pressing for civil rights).

☐ In elementary years, your child's motivations will reach more of a reciprocal "back-scratching" stage. During this period increase both your support and your expectations. Introduce him or her to mottos such as "If at first you don't succeed, try, try again," and the moral of Aesop's tortoise and hare fable: "Slow and steady wins the race." Underpin this with a discussion of the biblical principle of diligence—see Colossians 3:23; 2 Thessalonians 3:11-13; Ecclesiastes 10:18, 11:6; and Proverbs 10:4, 12:24, 13:4, and 22:29.

☐ Remain lavish in your praise and reward outstanding efforts. Remind your child of occasions when he or she followed through, and reaped the satisfaction of accomplishment. When your child fails to finish, make clear both your disappointment and your total support and love. Once again, offering help when your child is seriously frustrated or ready to quit is the best way to show support and model the discipline needed. And a consistent example in keeping your own commitments to your children is most important.

☐ In teen years, your child's motivations for following tasks should begin reflecting a more conscious and mature appreciation for the necessity of order in life. Expect your son or daughter to become consistent at basic chores, homework, taking care of possessions, and keeping promises. When the teenager fails, don't shield him or her from the resulting consequences. But don't remove your understanding, love, and support, either.

Of course, there's also a flip side to the discipline of following through. Sooner or later, all of us must give up on some things which we find to be beyond our abilities, overly demanding, or simply not enjoyable. So how does a child quit without becoming a quitter? Here are some principles to consider in forming the answer:

- Is there a natural quitting time? Can your child hold out until then? Sticking something out until the bitter end or until a natural cut-off point is a more positive choice than quitting at the moment of greatest stress, when difficulties are obscuring the end goal.
- Whose idea was the activity in the first place? If it wasn't your child's own choice, then abandoning it should be allowed more easily. If your child had begged to do it, be tougher.
- Was the commitment casually made? Help your child become fully aware of what may be involved in following through on a decision. This will yield a greater reluctance to give up when difficulties or fatigue arise.
- Are there exceptional circumstances in this case? Situations can change midstream. When your child wants to quit, ask lots of noncritical questions and listen "between the lines" for the negative factors discouraging him or her.

- Ask yourself, "Would it be called quitting if an adult were taking this action?"
- What will happen if the child isn't permitted to quit? Children need permission to back out when they've simply made a wrong choice, just as adults do. When we don't allow it, they adopt other undesirable behaviors, such as "forgetting," to cope with the pressure overload. It's better to help children behave responsibly while committed and then make a clean, honest, "I don't like it" or "I want out" break.

Your child can learn the discipline of following through. Few traits will be more important to his or her success as an adult—so don't neglect to follow through on this one!

25
KIDS AND AUTHORITY
BUILDING A POSITIVE VIEW

A recent bumper sticker declares, "Challenge Authority"—and many youths are doing just that. Concerned parents know that a child's attitudes and response patterns toward authority substantially impact his or her success, both now and as a future adult and parent. Building a balanced view isn't easy, but the following suggestions can help:

☐ Until the age of eight or nine, your youngster isn't capable of genuine abstract reasoning. His or her perceptions of authority are built from experience with parents and teachers, and the various rules of home, playground, and classroom.

☐ Build a positive view during these formative years by emphasizing fairness. Be as impartial as possible in the guidance and discipline you give. Fair discipline administered out of love builds self-esteem and will elicit a positive response. Arbitrary discipline, based on sheer power, tears down the child, and provokes reaction.

☐ In making and enforcing family rules, regularly discuss their two-fold purpose: protection from making bad mistakes and harm, and provision for making life's relationships more enjoyable. Your best opportunities are found in daily experiences. Disputes among neighborhood kids, for example, afford an ideal opportunity to talk about the role of rules, who has "authority" to make or change them, and what happens when they're violated. If your child is along when you receive a traffic citation, use the opportunity to explain why traffic laws are essential for safety and why violators including yourself, must be prosecuted. Keep the focus on the protection and blessing that underlie rules and authority.

☒ Consider your own attitude toward authority. Do you speak respectfully of your child's teachers and principal, the police, and government officials? Children naturally imitate their parents' attitudes toward authority.

☐ During later elementary years, help your child distinguish between various sources of authority:

1. *Absolute authority* is God's alone. He is our Creator, and there is no higher authority. Moral law begins with him. The laws of nature, for example, express his authority in the natural realm.

2. *Constitutional authority* derives from the consensus of those people living democratically under its control. Government, public education, the military, police and fire protection, and other public officials, servants, and representatives, have authority only because that power has been given to them.
3. *Delegated authority* is that conferred by a higher power. A policeman can make an arrest only because he has been given authority by a higher law and power. A stop sign carries no intrinsic authority, but we obey it because it represents an authority over us.

☐ As parents, our basic authority over our children is delegated by God. Take time to show your child in the Scriptures God's instructions to parents. The resulting insight can help them better understand your actions and discipline.

☐ Experience, character, and relationships are other common sources of authority. A person's advice is often valuable because he speaks from experience. The integrity and strength of a person's character can command authority. Jesus, for example, having set aside his divine power, still spoke with authority because of his personal character. And relationships often command authority. Witness how ruthlessly peer pressure modifies style of dress, speech, and a host of attitudes and behaviors in young people.

A positive view of authority built during your child's early years will help simplify your parenting when your adolescent begins internalizing his or her understanding of authority as a system of values and controls.

☐ During these years, your methods are modeling, dialogue, and a lot of "tongue biting" while your child makes those mistakes that teach life's lessons best.

☐ When your teenager asserts facts or observations to be true, a tactful "Says who?" can stimulate his or her ability to evaluate "authoritative" voices. Directing your child to Bible passages relevant to the issues will model a pattern important for the rest of his or her life.

☐ What about rebellion? Some stems from the normal process of establishing independence. And some is our fault, if we have wielded authority over our child as a personal defense mechanism—gaining power at the expense of affirming our child's personhood and need to make his or her own choices. Here, rebellion is actually healthy because the issue is not submission, but rather the abuse of authority.

☐ Other rebellion attempts to find its justification in rejecting society's values and appealing to different but carnal principles. Terrorism is a good example of this type of rebellion. Next time you view with your child a news report about terrorist activity, talk about the underlying view of authority. It could create a bridge for discussing what motivates rebellion in your child.

Giving your child a mature and balanced view of authority isn't easy. But little of real importance ever is. Success at it is certainly worth your effort!

26
WILL YOUR CHILD
RESPECT SIMPLICITY?

CONSUMERISM is a hallowed pillar of our society—and certainly no economy functions without consumers! But when our desire to consume warps our values and steals our hearts, it is at best a hollow passion. It destroys *simplicity*—that "single eye" toward God that results in an outward life-style free from the passion to possess.

As a parent who cares deeply about Christian values, you'll want to teach this important grace to your child. Admittedly, that's a tough assignment, since you must always model what you teach. But here are a few suggestions for building an appreciation for simplicity—beginning with its inward aspects:

☐ Contentment is foundational to simplicity. The apostle Paul said, "I have learned the secret of being content in any and every situation, whether well fed or hungry, whether living in plenty or in want. I can do everything through him who gives me strength" (Phil. 4:12, 13; Heb. 13:5, NIV). This attitude that "enough is enough," as Bishop John Taylor describes it, must underpin your efforts.

Young children are often the best teachers. They instinctively delight in simple joys more than in plastic toys. Follow their lead and turn a deaf family ear to the ad man's four-letter obscenities, "More, more, more!" Learn to enjoy together the simple pleasures that are already yours without cost: a sunrise, children's laughter, a good story, conversation with an old friend.

☐ Talk with your child about how simplicity leads to freedom, not bondage; how it makes life full rather than crowded; how it allows people to be valued above things. Focus conversation on the beauty, friendship, and simple joys around us.

☐ Encourage simplicity with plain and honest speech in your family. If you promise your child you'll be at a soccer game or violin recital, keep your word. To do otherwise is dishonest, and demonstrates duplicity rather than simplicity.

☐ Try to mean just what you say: For example, you may want to strike the expression "I'm starved" from your family vocabulary. At best it's only a half-truth, and obscures the fact that many people actually are starving. Do all you can to state what is actually the case without embellishment.

☐ Try to "live on a margin"—that is, to arrive a few minutes ahead of any scheduled appointment. If you have small children, this may at times require a miracle. But the practice will remove some frustration and anxiety from family life. Aim to arrive relaxed and ready for an event, rather than harried and tense.

☐ Work at cultivating regular moments of reflection. Encourage your child to read significant books to increase his understanding of himself and the world in which he lives. Kay Lindskoog's book *How to Grow a Young Reader* (David C. Cook, 1978) is an excellent resource. Establish a reading hour each evening for an older youngster. For a younger child, make it fifteen minutes to half an hour. Sometimes read to your child and discuss what you've read. "Existence clarification" is essential to defining who we are and what our purpose is for being.

Equally important to your child is the pursuit of outward simplicity. Consider these strategies:

☐ Help your child grow in self-control and self-government. Managing money is one practical area. Once it is determined what percentage of an allowance is to be given away and how much is to be saved (perhaps 10 percent for each), then decide together how the rest will be used, keeping an eye on the simplicity principle. (For a more complete discussion of allowances, see chapter 1.)

☐ As a family, discuss budget expenditures and establish a line beyond which you will not go. Recognize that our culture teaches both adults and children to desire everything in sight. Learning to buy what is needed rather than what is wanted is a difficult but freedom-giving skill.

☐ Revolt as a family against the propaganda machine in your home. Greet patently phony television commercials with a round of "Who do you think you're kidding?" comments.

☐ Help your child become acquainted with Christ's favorites—the poor and needy. Find situations in your neighborhood or town where your family can contribute some time and energy. Help sponsor an orphan child, and (without a "guilt trip") find small ways to become friends with those in need.

☐ Focus on homemade rather than "commercial" celebrations. There is an infinite variety of things to do that are great fun and draw you closer to one another. Make talk a big thing in your family. Delight in listening to each other's stories. Parents should become good at storytelling so they can set the pace.

The freedom of simplicity is tough to capture and tough to maintain with balance. But it rewards the diligent with a matchless joy in living. As Frances de Sales advised, "In everything, love simplicity."

PART THREE

VALUES

*A parent's responsibility
is not to his child's happiness;
it's to his character.*
Dr. Haim Ginott

*I would have you learn this great fact:
that a life of doing right
is the wisest life there is.*
Proverbs 4:11, TLB

27

HOW DO WE TEACH HONESTY?

HONESTY is one of the "core values," the real stuff of integrity and personal maturity. Like other values, it cannot be laid on a child like a coat of paint. Instead, it grows like grain in wood—part of the total development. As parents our task is to guide our children toward a strong conscience, a commitment to truth, and the ability to think for themselves.

Teaching honesty involves three levels of instruction: (1) the factual, (2) the relational, and (3) the personal.

- The *factual* level is the ongoing process of storing in your child's mind the concept of honesty and the consequences of dishonesty. Bible stories that illustrate the value of integrity are useful. Try telling elementary-age children the story of Jacob's lie to his father (Gen. 27). Discuss with teenagers the story of David's sin with Bathsheba (2 Sam. 11). Look at Josiah's faithfulness to God's plans (2 Kings 22, 23) and Micaiah's commitment to the truth (1 Kings 22:14).

- A child's psychosexual identity begins forming about the age of two. In addition to hearing what you say, he or she begins modeling you more closely. This desire to imitate begins the *relational* level of instruction. Consequently you'll need to look carefully at your own standards of honesty. Even a young child observes and understands much more than you realize about your commitment to integrity. What are you saying to your child, for example, by your business ethics and methods of reporting income for taxes? Do you ever tell "little white lies" to flatter someone or to avoid a small inconvenience (such as having a child tell a telephone caller you're not home)?

  It's important that your child see you honestly admitting to your own failures; for example, driving too fast in hazardous conditions, not arriving home when you said you would, or not keeping a promise. Such realistic modeling frees the child to struggle with his or her own honesty problems. One parent said that his kindergartner would never confess his sins to God in his bedside prayers until his dad began to confess openly his own shortcomings.

- The third level of training is to help the child *personalize* the principle of honesty in an everyday context. Show a preschooler or primary child a one-dollar bill and ask what he or she would do with it if it were found on the floor. Emphasize that being honest makes one feel good, helps others, and pleases God as well as Mom and Dad. Role play together other situations that would call for a decision to act honestly.

Keep in mind that according to research, a child in the earliest years has no internalized sense of right or wrong, only a fear of consequences. The child accepts what parents say because he or she wants to please. Praise versus a spanking or confinement to his or her room is the child's measure of an honest action, so ethical reasoning will have little effect on the behavior of a young child.

☐ By elementary age, however, the child's conscience has begun to mature, and actions are judged by internal moral standards. At this age honesty can be taught by telling true-to-life stories. Ask, for example, what the child would do if he or she saw a friend slip a small pencil sharpener into his lunch sack while in a stationery store. Follow with questions such as "Why?" and "What would result?" By this age, your child should have moved beyond the motivation of merely pleasing parents, and should be doing right things because it also makes the child happy with him or herself.

☐ Junior high and high school age children should have a well-developed conscience and should be thinking at more abstract levels about the values they hold. You can encourage this by discussing with your teenager newspaper articles that report various acts of dishonesty, both by individuals and by groups in business and government. Help your teenager discern the motivations for such acts.

☐ Continue to role play realistic situations appropriate to your child's age, such as opportunities to cheat on exams, using someone else's I.D. card, or lying to parents about where he or she has been. Speculate about the consequences of dishonesty, especially the damage it does to relationships. Note how one lie often leads to another in order to cover it up. Guide your child to see that without honesty, we can't get along with others in a healthy way—whether in school, home, marriage, community, or government.

If your child has developed a clear understanding of honesty rooted in Scripture, he or she will rise above the frequent trap of seeing right and wrong only in terms of what is most pleasurable, approved by others, or most expedient. The child's conscience will be sensitive to dishonesty in all its forms and will help him or her consistently avoid it.

☐ Throughout the development process, be sure to focus on

your child's actions as well as those of others. Affirm and praise the child, both alone and in front of his or her peers. Putting an honest label on your child will underscore that value and motivate him or her to live up to it when faced with the genuinely tough choices of life.

28

YOUR CHILD CAN TAME THE TV MONSTER

You know the statistics—by the time the average American child has finished high school, he or she will have spent some 15,000 hours watching TV. That's more time than doing anything else except sleeping. During those 15,000 hours, he or she will have been exposed to 350,000 commercials and watched 18,000 murders.

Television is perhaps the most pervasive force in our society. Nothing calls for you or your child to exercise more discernment than those moments you spend in front of the tube. Depending upon the viewing habits and amount of time spent, television can have either a very negative or a very positive effect upon your child.

On the negative side, too much TV, or TV watched without some parental guidance and training, can be harmful.

1. It can influence a child to want and buy things that are not good for him or her, or for which he or she has no genuine need.
2. It can become an escape from reality.
3. It can become a substitute for companionship and active play—inhibiting creativity and personal growth.
4. It can cause some children to become aggressive and even violent.
5. It can cause a child to have an unrealistic view of the world.

However, when used properly, TV can be beneficial.

1. It can bring a family together.
2. It can stimulate conversation between family members.
3. It can allow a child to relax and "unwind."
4. It can provide wholesome entertainment.
5. It can expose a child to new information, ideas, and perspectives.
6. It can expand a child's perception of the world.

These three questions are perhaps the most critical: (1) How much TV is OK? (2) Which types of programs should be avoided? (3) How do you build into your child discernment about what he or she sees on TV? Opinions vary, but several principles are widely acknowledged:

- No matter how much TV per day or week is allowed (some say one hour a day is the limit; others say up to four hours), it's not mentally healthy for any child to watch more than two hours at a time. Watching is a passive activity, and life is far more productive for those who live rather than observe it.
- Timing is just as important as the amount of viewing. Does your family's viewing disrupt meal times together or replace dinner conversation? Does it replace bedtime stories and

prayer? Does it squeeze out opportunities for evening family walks, games, or reading together?

☐ Make a survey of your family's viewing. Leave a chart on the set with spaces for each hour of the day for a week, to be filled in with the name of the program watched. You may be surprised by how much your family is watching, and the kinds of shows you spend the most time with.

☐ Try a family experiment. Agree to put the TV in the attic for a week (or even a month). Then plan lots of family activities for the evenings. Check out some library books and read together. Invest in some new board games. Take walks or "expeditions" around the neighborhood. Plant a garden; paint a room; do anything that will be productive and fun as a family. The first few days going "cold turkey" will be rough, but soon you'll be amazed at how much time you have! At the end of the trial period you'll be able to make a more objective, less emotional estimate of how much time your family should spend viewing the TV.

☐ The mental anguish a child can suffer as a result of watching TV comes largely from commercials, TV violence, and the unrealistic way in which TV often portrays life. To compensate for this and correct your child's developing ways of thinking, you need to view programs together so that you can discuss the fallacies and inconsistencies you observe. After a program, talk about what you saw while it's still fresh in your minds:

1. Expose the assumptions and values behind commercials.
2. Point out violence, and talk about the seriousness of violent behavior in real life.
3. Counter stereotypes by challenging the standard TV images of women, men, families, ethnic groups, and religious groups.
4. Look for political and social bias in the way TV news is presented. Talk about how hundreds of news items could be reported each day, but only a few can be chosen, making subtle distinctions between what's "important" and what's not. Think about the newscaster's choice of words, sometimes emotionally loaded.

☐ Make TV watching purposeful by sitting down with the program guide at the beginning of the week and deciding with your child which programs are worth watching. Set the limits together. Use these questions as guidelines for worthwhile viewing:

1. Is the program either interesting or entertaining?
2. Can the child understand it?
3. Does it show a clear difference between right and wrong, and does it teach worthwhile values?
4. Will it be frightening?
5. Does it make a clear distinction between reality and fantasy?

☐ For a young child, rule out programs that have crime as a major theme, leave stress unresolved, focus on fear, or give a fuzzy distinction between fantasy and reality.

☐ Keep in mind that the standard "adult programming" period after 9:00 P.M. is not intended for children.

☐ Parents who are TV addicts themselves cannot expect their children to control their watching. You must model the attitudes toward TV you want your child to have.

Your children can become discerning about TV viewing. Trust God for wisdom and wade into the battle. The TV doesn't have to be a monster in your home.

29

WHAT IS YOUR CHILD LEARNING ABOUT SEX?

HUMAN sexuality is one of the most exploited and bankrupt aspects of our culture. Crowded counseling centers, skin magazines, and even bathroom graffiti confirm this. Helping your children gain and practice a balanced and biblical view of sexuality is a difficult assignment, and one you might be tempted to leave to "professionals."

But parents are in the best position to teach children about sex. They're the first to field questions from the youngster that have arisen in natural situations (such as a baby sibling's bath), and they have the child's best interests at heart. Parents can also provide a positive context of warmth and love in which healthy attitudes toward sexuality can be cultivated.

At the same time, sex education is such a critical part of your child's development that it should never be left to teachers or peers. Yet in a survey of teenagers some years ago, only one in fourteen kids had received sex information from their parents before they learned it from friends! The result is widespread misinformation and unhealthy attitudes.

At the outset, we must recognize that a person's attitudes about sex are always tied to his level of emotional maturity and sense of self-esteem. So consideration of some basic developmental principles is important in order to match the strategies for learning to a child's readiness:

- Your youngster's response to sexual urges will rise out of his experiences with life and love in general. By providing a positive and supportive emotional climate in your home, you convey that psychological intimacy and personal involvement are not to be feared—essential ingredients for developing a healthy attitude about sex.
- The attitudes your child has toward his or her body will color the child's view of sex. From your comments, "looks," and responses to your child's questions and self-explorations, he or she will develop feelings largely the same as the ones you have about your own body. This is an area of crucial concern in the earliest years.
- Friendly feelings between your child and the parent of the opposite sex will substantially condition his or her enjoyment of the other sex, as well as future sexual adjustments. The pleasure and open affection you and your spouse display toward each other is also essential modeling.
- Handling discipline in your home in a democratic way is important for positive sex education. The mutual respect, involvement, and commitment family democracy stresses will become a part of your child's sexual values too.

Here are some practical ways to give your child a healthy view of sexuality:

☐ Beginning with your preschooler's first questions, give him accurate and truthful information about the reproductive process. Decide on the names you'll use for body parts and processes. Your public library should have books that guide you in talking to your child at every age level. Answer specific questions with specific facts. The basic guideline here is to give an accurate answer, but don't try to strive for an in-depth or comprehensive response that entails much more than your child wants to know at the moment. Keep it simple.

☐ A preadolescent youngster, through contacts with pets and peers, will find many occasions for questions. You'll need to be correcting misinformation and gently countering unhealthy peer attitudes. At the same time, a child needs to prepare for the changes that will be taking place in his or her body and emotions. Explain that sexual urges will be powerful. Listen to your child's ideas and attitudes about sex before giving him or her the facts. You can then best clear up the misconceptions he or she may have picked up from others and his or her own imaginings.

☐ To an adolescent, point out the differences between male and female sexual urges. A girl should know that boys are primarily stimulated visually and are aroused much more quickly than girls. A boy should know that a girl's sexual urges are more frequently associated with romantic love and that his advances will easily be interpreted as evidence of enduring love.

☐ If you feel discomfort in discussing sex, be honest with your youngster. Make it clear that the subject is legitimate, but that your past training is responsible for your lack of ease. Learning and practicing the names of sexual organs and functions beforehand can help.

☐ Work hard at keeping open, easy communication with your child. Make active, empathetic listening your goal. Avoid lectures like the plague. Your youngster's sense that you understand his or her predicaments is invaluable.

☐ If your child should fail at sexual control, point him or her to the forgiveness available in Jesus Christ. Make sure you forgive as well. In adolescence, when sexual urges and peer pressure are intense, the best insulation against indiscriminate sexual behavior is a high degree of self-worth.

Obviously, a great variety of factors affect how your youngster will handle his or her sexuality. Your prayers and commitment to intelligent, sensitive, and balanced parenting can give your child the healthy view of sex he or she deserves and needs.

30

WHAT ARE KIDS' RIGHTS?

CIVIL rights, minority rights, women's rights, student rights—you can hardly move, it seems, without infringing on the rights of someone or something. And now we hear about kids' rights?

If you're hesitant to read on, it's understandable. But a concern for "rights" is a fundamental value most of us hold and want to pass on to our children. If you don't think so, just recall the last time someone tried to limit one of your own freedoms.

Somehow, when it comes to kids, human rights seem to fade behind the (legitimate) principle of parental authority. Often we parents dismiss our children's rights without discussion or consideration because of the fine line between their "rights" and our responsibility.

Nevertheless, many negative reactions and resentments, and defiant and rebellious attitudes in children stem from a sense that their rights are being violated. Witness the common protests from kids these days: "I have a right to ..."; "Why can't I decide ...?"

Defining a child's rights within a family may be a bit difficult, but doing it together can be an extremely rewarding process. Here are a few "rights" to consider including:

☐ The right to be a child—not a little adult. Childhood isn't just "wasted time" until a person grows up. In fact, we should hope that certain facets of the child in us will stay active as long as we live. But frequently we parents become so concerned about preparing our children for adult life and the "real world" that we fail to give them permission to enjoy the precious years of childhood. The right to be a child—to be just who he or she is now—is essential to wholeness. Each child needs the freedom to grow up as the unique, one-of-a-kind, unrepeatable miracle that he or she is.

☐ The right to play. Play is more important than we realize. It's the child's work. It's his or her job to crawl, build with blocks, make mud pies, empty drawers, skateboard, or surf. Becoming good at play is just as important as becoming good at making the bed, cleaning the room, mowing the lawn, or emptying the trash. Perhaps it is more out of jealousy than principle that we parents often convey the idea that play is a privilege to be tolerated only after the real work is done.

☐ What about the right to have a say in family matters? Children understandably want to be included in the process that decides what happens to them, and it is especially important to children ten years of age and older. In fact, the right to be heard is essential to developing a healthy self-image. And participation in decisions yields a greater willingness to share in the responsibility for the outcome.

This is not to say, of course, that parents should hand over their authority to their children. But it's possible to be in charge while still allowing kids a meaningful role in the decision-making process by genuinely listening to their opinions and preferences, and then taking those into consideration.

☐ The right to privacy. Many parents unfortunately believe they have the right to open their children's mail, read their private diaries, borrow their belongings without first asking permission, or enter their rooms without first knocking on the door. If anyone failed to respect our own privacy in these ways, we'd probably be offended, and rightly so. Why shouldn't our children deserve the same respect?

The violation of a child's right to privacy for his or her own body is the first step toward incest, a concern of frightening proportions in homes of every economic status, according to recent research.

☐ The right to a "fair trial" before punishment. Every child should have the chance to defend his or her innocence before being disciplined. Circumstances of which we're unaware might make a difference in our response to the misbehavior.

☐ Here are some other rights to consider for your child: the right to be treated fairly; to be loved; to be appreciated; to say no sometimes; to hold an opinion different from yours; to be forgiven for mistakes; to be discipled in your faith; to say what he or she thinks respectfully; to change his mind sometimes; to be him or herself and not a mere extension of your ego. In short, we should extend to our children many of the basic rights we reserve for ourselves!

If you're a parent who tends to feel that kids have no rights because they're too young or haven't yet earned them, think again. It's far better that your children learn the principle of rights from you than from some other source.

At the same time, there's no better place than home to learn the responsibilities that accompany rights, and the difference between rights and privileges. Too often we hear today of people who claim a "right" that is really just a license to act discourteously, irresponsibly, or immorally (such as the "right" to blow cigarette smoke in the face of someone next to them in line in a public place). The old saying "My rights end where yours begin" is a principle worth learning at home.

Others demand privileges or support from society that are not rights, but rather gifts. Our children must learn that others don't owe them a livelihood, and that the rights of citizenship come with commitments as well.

Why not call a first meeting of the "Family Council" and, after considerable discussion, draft a "Family Bill of Rights and Responsibilities"? Clarifying rights as well as godly lines of authority can cultivate a fresh, beautiful spirit of cooperation within your family.

31

FAMILY TRADITIONS ARE WORTH THE EFFORT!

Traditions are the threads from which our most valued memories are woven. According to social scientists who study the family, traditions make a significant difference in our lives by creating and reinforcing emotional security in the home. In fact, some studies have shown that the families with the strongest ties have the most traditions, and that ritual is a symbol of how family members feel about one another.

Actually, customs can strengthen families in a number of ways. First of all, traditions establish continuity. They tie the present to the past, linking one year to the next and bridging the generations.

Family stability is another benefit of traditions. The regular, familiar patterns of consistent family customs—whether nightly bedtime stories or table grace before every meal—add a predictability to the cycle of family life that's both comfortable and comforting.

Yet another reward of traditions is the sense of family identity they cultivate. Children today are constantly pressured by the media to identify with their peers instead of their families. But special customs at home help make a family unique and give its members a feeling of belonging.

Closely related to this benefit is the spirit of family unity traditions build. Think, for example, of the warm closeness each person feels when family members are together for the traditional Thanksgiving dinner. Traditions cultivate a sense of oneness that endures even long after the children are grown and have moved away.

Finally, traditions enrich our lives with meaning by setting aside the average routine and focusing on what's important to us. It's easy to let normal days slip by unnoticed—but when we observe special days and events, we have a chance to pause and reflect on our lives. Birthdays, for example, remind us of the growth and uniqueness of each family member; wedding anniversaries call attention to the deepening love in our marriage. And holidays such as Christmas and Easter give us opportunities to think about our faith and values, and to share them with our children.

In all these respects, you can strengthen your home by strengthening your traditions. If you find that one of your traditional observances has lost its meaning, or if you want to start some new ones, here are some ideas:

☐ Begin by asking your family these questions: First, what traditions have been carried on from the generations before us? (You may want to involve the grandparents in answering this one.) Next, ask how did our family's new traditions develop?

And third, what new traditions would we like to add? Or, perhaps, what old ones would we like to reestablish?

Now, as you evaluate together your present traditions and plan new ones, keep these guidelines in mind:

☐ Remember that simple customs are best. Elaborate or expensive rituals can become difficult to maintain.

☐ Plan and prepare well ahead of time—sometimes weeks or even months. This builds anticipation that's also an important part of the fun. Avoid canceling or changing traditions on the spur of the moment.

☐ Choose traditions that focus on values and people rather than costly gifts or activities.

☐ Make sure every family member is included in both the preparation and the observance.

☐ Don't be pressured or rigid—enforcing a tradition takes the fun out of it. If an idea doesn't work, try a different one next time.

☐ Use the time as a "teachable moment" to call attention to the significance of the occasion. What better time to tell your children about God's love than on Christmas Eve? Or how about talking with teens about romance and marriage on your anniversary?

☐ Finally, if your family's ready to add some new traditions, ideas can come from many sources. Talk to grandparents and older relatives, especially if they're from "the old country." Ask other families what traditions they observe and why. Look for ideas in the novels you read or movies you watch. You can even check out library books on customs in other lands.

Consider some of these suggestions:

☐ On birthdays, why not gather the family first thing in the morning around the birthday person's bed for a rousing rendition of the birthday song? Then decorate his or her place at the breakfast table with balloons, crepe paper, and cards.

☐ For wedding anniversaries, take a family portrait or photo each year in front of the very same background as a record of the family's growth.

☐ Christmas offers a whole season full of warm tradition possibilities. One idea is to choose a significant family event from the past twelve months that you'd like to remember. Then make or purchase a tree ornament that symbolizes the event. A toy kitten, for example, could represent a new pet, or a tiny boat, this year's vacation. Be sure to paint or carve the year on each one. Years from now, your Christmas tree will be a family "history book."

☐ At Thanksgiving, some families tell the story of the Pilgrims before the big meal. Then, as a small basket is passed around, each person drops in two kernels of dried corn and with each shares something he or she is most thankful for.

☐ Remember that traditions don't have to be yearly events. A good weekly custom is for Dad to give Mom a rest by preparing Sunday breakfast with help from the kids. And bedtimes and mealtimes are perfect moments for daily traditions.

These ideas should be starters to help you think of some traditions that are perfectly suited to your family. With a little imagination and preparation, family traditions will become family treasures. And best of all, the reward for your efforts—strong family ties—will endure even across the years and the miles.

32

ON LEARNING THE VALUE OF THINGS

WHAT parent hasn't been upset upon finding toys strewn across a child's bedroom floor, or that expensive new sweater in a heap next to the dresser along with dirty socks and underwear? Instantly you're ready to lecture on stewardship for the forty-fifth time!

The Scriptures, high replacement costs, and the limited natural resources of this planet all dictate that we must not waste or abuse the things we have. At the core of the matter is the issue of stewardship. So let's look first at some important principles and then at ways they can be instilled in your children:

- We need to keep in mind that in a society as loaded with material possessions as ours, gaining a perspective on the value of things is difficult. For most of our children, "easy come, easy go" is a functional reality. Jesus often warned about the deceit of riches and the blindness that can accompany wealth.

- God has promised to supply all our *needs* but not all our *wants*. Unfortunately, consumer advertising is quite sophisticated at creating within us "felt needs"—desires for non-essentials that masquerade as essentials. This consumer attitude, combined with immaturity and intense peer pressure among children, makes it difficult for children to understand and practice a balanced view of stewardship.

- Since values are better caught than taught, modeling for your child a proper use and care of things is essential. Ask yourself what attitudes your child is learning from your spending habits and maintenance of possessions.

- Most items have an inherent lifespan. Good stewardship involves treating them so they are useful the full length of that time. A pattern of ruining or destroying possessions before their lifespan is over reflects a poor sense of values.

- Many products these days (including toys) are so poorly made that they break or wear out too quickly. A child should not be allowed to feel guilt or undue frustration over a toy that breaks more from poor engineering than from abusive treatment. As parents we should exercise good stewardship in judging the quality of the toys and things we buy.

- People are always more important than things. The preservation of your child's feelings, self-esteem, and personhood is far more important than the preservation of his or her things or yours, no matter how hard you have worked for them. It's easy to come down hard on a child when he or she breaks or loses a toy, all the while forgetting that the loss is really the child's. A better approach is to deal with the sense of loss instead of focusing so much on your own frustrations. Balance at this point is difficult, but essential.

To help your child develop understanding about the value of things and to build good habits of stewardship, try these ideas:

☐ Limit the number of things your child has to be concerned with. When he or she is overloaded with toys, it's impossible for the child to see each one as valuable. Try rotating toys, putting some things away for a while so that they're "new" when brought out again.

☐ Help your child work to earn some of the things he or she wants. When your child understands the effort it takes to acquire an item, he or she will value it more highly.

☐ Talk with your child about our earth's natural resources and where plastics, metals, wood, and paper come from. Discuss the meaning of nonrenewable resources.

☐ If your child is old enough to understand how to handle and care for possessions and, after a warning, continues to be abusive or careless with something, suspend use of it for a period of time. Enjoyment of things is a privilege, not a right.

☐ If something is broken or ruined through abuse or neglect, have the child pay for the repairs or replacement through his or her own earnings.

☐ If toys, clothes, and other possessions are constantly left lying around, create a Saturday Box. Anything left lying around out of place goes in the box and can't be retrieved till Saturday. It will seem cruel, but a week or two of this practice will work wonders in changing habits.

☐ Teach respect for the possessions of others by establishing guidelines in your home for use of another's belongings. Include rules about asking permission to borrow and repairing or replacing borrowed items that are damaged or used up.

☐ Through books, films, missionary literature, and some family outings, expose your family to people who have much less than you do. Consider how each member of your family can share your abundance with those less fortunate.

☐ Examine advertisements together as a family to discover

hidden assumptions, values, or manipulation. Discuss how luxury items are made to appear as "necessities" for maintaining our status, attractiveness, intelligence, popularity, convenience, or comfort.

☐ If you find you're simply laden down with too many things, clean house. Give some of them away, or have a garage sale and contribute the proceeds to a worthy cause. Encourage every family member to participate in the housecleaning.

Above all, hold your possessions in an open hand. They can support, but never create, a genuinely rich life.

33

DO YOUR CHILDREN KNOW THEIR ROOTS?

A bestseller made into two TV spectaculars has prompted almost everyone in America to wonder about his roots. The program uncovered a deep need in the lives of many people in our society who have been uprooted, both geographically and socially. Years of rebellion against traditions, dishonor for older people, and fractured family life have finally resulted in an emptiness that cries out to be filled.

No doubt about it—a sense of heritage is important to all of us, and especially to children. Strong self-identity (knowing who you are) is essential to mental health and a sense of worth. And much of our identity comes from our family, both immediate and past.

The same is true spiritually. We gain strength and identity from the family of God and through the stories of our spiritual forefathers recorded in the Bible and church history. Evidently God thought physical and spiritual lineages were important enough to record them carefully in the Bible. Our roots *are* important!

Tracing your family roots can be a rewarding and fascinating project. Every search should start with information about members of your immediate family—and recording these details is more than worth the effort, even if it goes no further.

Alex Haley, the author of *Roots*, described the process in the September 1977 issue of *Parents* magazine:

What this means, specifically, is getting down those trunks from the attic, or wherever the old photos, clothes and diaries are stored, and sharing those treasures with the kids. Talk about the way it used to be, the things you did, the kind of entertainment you enjoyed, the clothes you wore. If there are grandparents or even great-grandparents in the family, urge them to tell your children stories of their past, about when they were children. . . . Kids are hungry for this kind of information, for recreation of lives they can identify with and feel a part of.

☐ To begin searching out your family roots, get a large looseleaf notebook. Then visit and talk to as many relatives as possible. Collect all the old photos, newspaper clippings, and family artifacts you can find. Write everything down.

☐ Start by having yourself and each family member write about themselves. (Take dictation from small children.) Imagine you are writing a letter to some future grandson or great-granddaughter. Try to include details in each of the following categories where appropriate.

1. *Early family life.* Tell about your earliest memories, pets, favorite toys, places, and friends. Describe your home and family traditions and celebrations.
2. *Homes.* List the places you have lived since birth and the neighbors you knew well. Describe the house, yards, and neighborhoods that were yours, and give a short description of the town.
3. *School.* Record your best and worst memories from school days, including any teacher(s) who may have influenced you deeply. What were your best and worst subjects? What extracurricular activities did you take part in? Did you receive any honors or awards?
4. *Marriage and family.* Describe how you met your spouse, your courtship and wedding. Say what qualities most attracted you to him or her. Then tell about your children—details surrounding their births, special memories from their early years, and the difficulties and joys you've experienced with them.
5. *Occupations.* List the work training and experiences you've had, including any time spent in military service. Remember to add any awards you've received for work performance. Tell how you chose your career, and talk about reasons for making changes in vocational direction.
6. *Personal notes.* Talk about yourself and your life-style: your ambitions, feelings, greatest thrills, dreams, disappointments, and failures.
7. *Friends, social life, and leisure time.* Tell which friendships have meant the most to you. Talk about vacations, hobbies, reading preferences, and other spare-time pursuits.
8. *Religion and philosophy of life.* Explain the conclusions you have reached about the value and meaning of life. Describe your spiritual beginnings, significant moments of insight, and the church communities you've been part of.

9. *Health.* Describe your physical appearance and major illnesses, especially any that may have hereditary origins. Talk about what you eat and how you exercise.

10. *Public life.* List the civic and other organizations to which you've belonged, any offices held, and the times you've appeared in the news.

11. *Financial resources.* List a typical month's budget and your history of wages and credit practices.

Several books are available containing helpful suggestions, forms, and charts. A good one is *Your Family Tree* by William R. Jordan, III (Golden Press).

☐ As your interest grows, gather more photographs and try to get oral histories on tape from relatives. As you do, take special note of the traditions and character strengths you find that reinforce the values you wish your children to have. Knowing that one of their ancestors was a man or woman of faith, courage, or hard work will give them pride in carrying on the tradition.

☐ Frame photos of family members as far back as possible and create a "family history wall" in your home. Talk often, especially with young children, about who the people are and the important facts about them.

☐ As your notebook grows, make copies that the children will keep and continue in their own homes someday. Take care to preserve the things you wish your grandparents and great-grandparents had preserved. Your grandchildren will love you for it. After all, *you* are their roots!

34
WILL YOUR CHILD
UNDERSTAND PRIVACY?

GIVING your child privacy
means surrendering your "right to know" everything he or she
thinks and does. And that can be threatening. But right to

privacy is an important value to acquire; it affirms crucial self-confidence and worth. So a healthy child will need to respect and handle privacy on at least these four levels:

1. Personal space and belongings—having one's own room, desk drawer, closet shelf, box, or diary, and respecting similar spaces and belongings of others.
2. Physical isolation—being comfortable when apart from other people—the art of being alone without being lonely.
3. Mental solitude—holding and enjoying one's private thoughts and feelings as special.
4. Modesty—the privacy appropriate to one's body.

☐ Early lessons in privacy begin with the concept of "yours" and "mine." A preschooler's toys and bed are usually his or her first encounters with privacy. Unfortunately, under the premise of learning to share, we often force a child to surrender that privacy. At this stage, it's a good idea to hold back two or three special toys that are not shared with friends who come to play. They can be private.
☐ As a child grows into the elementary years, his or her need for privacy and the respect for others' privacy grows. Learning to keep secrets is one stage of growth. Respecting the private possessions, times, and places of other family members is another. (This is especially important when siblings share a room.) Becoming aware of appropriate physical modesty is yet another.
☐ During this time, violations of privacy should receive the same consistent discipline as dishonesty or theft. When your child is nine or ten and capable of abstract reasoning, explain that stealing people's privacy is the same as stealing their goods.

While the emphasis during early years is on the privacy of treasured possessions, your child will gradually replace these with treasured and private thoughts, dreams, and conversations with you, other friends, and God. His or her motivation to protect and enjoy privacy in these ways will increase.

During adolescence, you'll need to balance your continuing

eagerness to share deeply in your child's world with his or her need for emotional distance—to hold more thoughts, feelings, and activities as private. While it can be a difficult time, especially if the relationship has not been solid over the prior years, here are some important guidelines:

☐ Be a student of your teenager. Watch for clues that he or she wants to talk. You'll develop a healthier closeness this way than if you pry or pressure your child to open up.

☐ You can signal your continuing commitment to the right to privacy by showing it yourself. Knock before entering your child's room. Ask permission before you borrow a book or some other possession. Never open a child's mail, go through his or her desk or dresser drawers, or read a private journal. These are merely the same courtesies you would extend to other adults and would expect to receive yourself. And showing respect this way will open doors far more successfully than forcefully busting them down.

☐ When privacy is invaded in your family or a violation of privacy is reported in the news, talk about it. Leading questions, such as "Did that person have the right to know?" or "What was wrong with the action?" can help your child think through the issues and better decide when curiosity is appropriate and when it is not.

☐ Make your child aware of the privileges of privacy guaranteed under our Constitution. Read together a discussion of this right in an encyclopedia. Talk about the potential uses of information and abuses of privacy that modern computer technology is making possible. Talk about credit histories and other files containing personal information, and to what extent these files should be open to public review.

☐ Help your teenager keep privacy in perspective. Point out that to be psychologically and spiritually healthy, we all need to blend our lives with others, and to have at least some relationships with a healthy intimacy. Privacy should not result in a "leave me alone" attitude. To care about people requires letting them past many of our mental and emotional defenses.

☐ Intimacy with God is also critical. Point out that God inter-
cepts our thoughts even before we think them (Ps. 139).
Though we have no secrets from him, he still respects our
right to free choice, even when we use it to choose against
him.

In a society of burgeoning information and eroding restraints
on its use, the balanced view of privacy your child gains will
be an important strength in his or her character. The best
lessons your child will learn about this value and others will
all take place in the privacy of your own home.

35
YOU CAN INSTILL COURAGE IN YOUR CHILD

ONE of the saddest characteristics of many of today's youth is their willingness to remain on the fringes of life, avoiding the risks of exploring it to its very essence. Many parents do no better. "Living the good life," wrote Nikolai Berdyaev, "is frequently dull and flat and commonplace. Our greatest problem is to make it fiery and creative and capable of spiritual struggle." In short, we need *courage*.

If courage is the price of admission to life at its deeper levels, why is it so hard to engage? Perhaps it's because courage is difficult to define. The word *courage* comes from the Middle English *corage*, and the Old French *cuer*, meaning "heart." And just as the heart keeps the body alive by pumping blood to the arms, legs, and head, so courage is a source of substance and energy for all the areas of life.

How will your child become infused with courage? Can it be taught in a classroom, or taken in a tablet like vitamins? Obviously not. Like any other value, it must be learned by example. Here, then, are some ways that courage is caught:

☐ First of all, children (and adults) need to realize there's no disgrace in experiencing fear; it's a normal feeling that everyone has from time to time. Courage doesn't mean the absence of fear—it means acting *in spite of fear*. The difference between courage and cowardice is the difference between facing a danger and running from it.

☐ Begin teaching courage by dealing first with the specific fears your child has. A young child may be afraid of the dark, animals, noises, abandonment, or strangers. An older child may fear rejection by peers, failure, bereavement, or (according to recent surveys) nuclear holocaust.

☐ Whatever the child's fear, *naming it* is the first step to facing it bravely. Help your child identify fears by asking questions that explore the reasons behind fearful behaviors you've observed: unwillingness to enter a darkened room alone; excessive worry about "what my friends think of me"; frequent references to the divorce of a friend's parents.

☐ If the fear is a physical one (such as fear of a dog or the dark), try approaching it together—but don't force the issue with an unwilling child. Of course, calling the child names like "chicken" or "fraidy cat" only makes matters worse. Let the child take his or her time, over a period of days or weeks if necessary, to approach the object of fear gradually. Praise the child's courage as you watch it grow.

☐ If the fear is an intangible one (such as fear of bereavement) you'll need to talk realistically about the matter, without denying that the event or situation feared could possibly happen. (The child usually knows it's possible no matter what you say.) You can talk about the improbability of such an event, but you need to discuss how your child and the family would cope with it.

☐ At this point your own faith in God's love is critical. Your child needs to see that your confidence in facing the future, whatever happens, is based on your conviction that he is in control. It *is* a terrifying world in many ways, with an uncertain future—but we can live with courage because of God's promise to make us "more than conquerors" in every circumstance.

☐ Beyond helping a child face his or her specific fears, we need to stretch the child's capacity for courage by placing him or her in challenging situations. Courage is deepened only in the context of risk and the possibility of failure.

Controlled physical risk situations offer one of the best ways to build courage, because we can be pushed to our physical limits rather quickly. (Just see, for starters, how many push-ups you can do!) Of course, reaching our emotional and spiritual limits can take a great deal more time.

☐ Try putting a pair of boxing gloves on your child. In only a few seconds one good "bonk" on the nose will offer a fine opportunity to discuss what courage is about. Or try offering a reward your child wants very much for the completion of a marathon calibrated to challenge his or her physical limits. Talk about what it took to succeed, or why failure was the result.

☐ Join your older child in a lesson some Saturday morning by having your spouse drop you off without any money quite a few miles from home. Your assignment: to get home before dark. The ensuing controlled stress situation will afford ample time to talk about practical courage.

☐ Follow up experiences like these with evening or dinner table discussions of incidents from the newspaper that demonstrate courage in action. Ask questions such as: What would *you* have done in that situation? How would you feel if you had taken a risk and failed? What's the most difficult thing you've ever done? What's the most challenging thing I could ever ask you to do?

Opportunities to display courage confront us and our children in several areas. Here are three primary ones:

1. *Decisions.* What a child becomes is largely a matter of the choices he or she makes. Difficult decisions take courage both to make and to maintain. Choosing what's right amid the confusion, temptation, and conflict of our day can require extraordinary courage.

2. *Commitments.* It takes courage to be an individual—to stand alone, if necessary, not only for what's right, but also for our own uniqueness. It's especially tough when peer pressure is strong. In fact, your child's courage to be who he or she really is may be the basis for all other forms of courage.

3. *Caring actions.* Rollo May, in his book *The Courage to Create,* says, "The most prevalent form of cowardice in our time hides behind the statement, 'I did not want to become involved.'" Ours is an age of apathy, and our children must gain the courage to be involved in the needs of the world around them.

Several years ago, a magazine survey of teenagers revealed that most would rather settle for low success than high risk of failure. Your child doesn't have to be one of them.

36

WILL YOUR CHILD LOVE THE ARTS?

ARE the arts merely a leisure-time activity of the rich? Our culture's tilt toward science and technology might suggest that conclusion. But history clearly answers no. Most of what we cherish about other people we have learned through their music, paintings, crafts, architecture, and literature. The arts are a window to the soul and a sign that we're made in the image of a creative God. For those reasons alone our children need to develop an appreciation for the arts to be balanced and whole people.

While it's important to expose your child to styles and media beyond just those that appeal to you, you don't need to be an expert to help your child learn to love the arts. Regular exposure and hands-on experiences are the essential ingredients. And lots of fun will be added to your family dynamics in the process.

For exposure consider these ideas:

☐ Research your area's cultural resources. Most communities have local performing groups in theater and dance, orchestras, art galleries, museums, and perhaps an art guild or an annual festival. Local schools or colleges are excellent resources. Keep an eye on the newspaper for announcements of upcoming events sponsored by schools. The cost is usually less than a sports event, and often admission is free.

☐ As a family, visit an exhibit or performance every month or two. Or go one-on-one with a child for an unforgettable "date." Be sure to follow it up with conversation about what you saw or heard. Ask questions about what each family member liked best and why, and then express your own perspectives. If a particular musical piece was a hit, you may want to locate and purchase a recording of it for a birthday or Christmas gift. A print of a favorite painting may be available framed as a poster, or in a book about the artist.

☐ Check with your local chamber of commerce or local art guild for names of working artists in your area. Visit musicians, painters, or sculptors in their studios while they rehearse or create. Most will welcome a brief chance to share with an interested child, and you'll relish the treat as well. Your child might even begin to develop an interest and talent in a particular medium as a result of the visit! In fact, a breadth of exposure to the arts will allow a child to discover early those areas of greatest interest to him or her.

For hands-on experiences try these:

☐ Encourage your preschooler to experiment by providing raw materials, such as simple musical instruments or water-based paints with big brushes. Praise the child's "masterpieces" and post them on a family bulletin board, put them under the glass top of a coffee table, or cover them with clear contact paper to make breakfast placemats.

Spread a plastic cloth on the table or under a tree outside and let the child experiment with clay. If you can locate a kiln, use ceramic clay and have the best results fired to keep on a bookshelf.

☐ Encourage an older child to use and develop his or her skills of observation and drawing. Notice together sculptures, fountains, and murals in shopping centers and parks. Let the child sketch while you shop. If your child is a professed non-artist, pick up a copy of the book *Drawing on the Right Side of the Brain* by Betty Edwards (J.P. Tarcher, 1979). The author is an art teacher who has discovered a way to teach anyone to draw with remarkable skill. You may want to learn a new skill yourself.

☐ Encourage your child to take art, music, and creative writing courses in school, and to participate in literary, theatrical, musical, or other artistic extracurricular activities.

☐ Take an art class or learn to play a musical instrument along with your child. Who wouldn't be thrilled at that kind of support and encouragement from a parent? The rapport it builds will be priceless.

☐ Make your home an art appreciation studio. Read together frequently from classical literature: poetry, plays, stories, and, with older children, novels. Decorate with inexpensive prints of great paintings and cast miniatures of great sculptures. Invest in some classical music recordings to listen to together. Ask the librarian and the art and music teachers at school for recommendations in all these areas. Often records and even framed prints can be borrowed from your local library. Check out classics, and primers on art, music, and literature to study together. Have good books (especially those with full-color reproductions of fine art) available for browsing throughout the house.

☐ Watch television listings for productions of plays, concerts, and other special performances. Public TV has many fine offerings in this regard. Watch them together, and take time afterward to hold a family "critic's corner."

☐ Start a family fund to which each person contributes earnings for the purchase each year of some piece of original art—

perhaps a painting, sculpture, or stained glass window. The project will keep art appreciation in focus for all of you.

☐ As with any value, we must model what we say if the message is to be heard. Make sure your own commitment to the value of the arts is solid before you involve your child. Or admit that it's a new interest for you, and you can learn together.

Either way the message will be plain: In this family we want to be whole persons who enjoy and appreciate all the capacities God gives each of us, including artistic gifts. At home, art appreciation is never a waste of time.

37
TREAT YOUR CHILD TO GOOD HEALTH

IT'S curious. Interest in exercise and nutrition is at an all-time high. Yet convenience foods in increasing proportions appear on street corners and in grocery freezers. Weight control products and salons are booming because we aren't really practicing the fundamentals of maintaining good health.

Life patterns for good nutrition and physical exercise often begin at home, so it's up to us as parents to set the pace. While most children are taught in school the basics of the four food groups, exercise, and rest, the lessons are daily offset by a devastating barrage of media messages promoting sugar-loaded cereals, pastries, soft drinks, and candies.

Although by no means exhaustive, here are some suggestions for helping your child find a natural enthusiasm for good food and exercise:

☐ Begin by evaluating the role of sugar in your home. Do you consume a lot of high-sugar items for dessert and between-meal snacks? Keep in mind the principle, what you buy is what you eat! Good nutrition begins in the grocery shopping cart.

☐ Since snacks and school lunch bags are where many children consume a great deal of excess sugar, consider healthful alternatives to sweets, such as peanuts, raisins, dried fruits, fresh fruits and juices, trail mixes, and popcorn. An excellent Orange Julius type drink can be made by mixing in a blender one quart of orange juice, a teaspoon of vanilla, one tablespoon of honey, six ice cubes, and an optional egg.

☐ Another family habit to evaluate is the role of refined sugar in rewards and celebrations. There's nothing wrong with sweets at occasional holiday celebrations and birthday parties. But if you regularly reward good behavior with candy or other sugar items, a harmful sugar addiction can result.

☐ Your perceptions of sugar intake can be dramatically heightened if you review the ingredients list required by law on food products. Ingredients are listed according to their percentage of the total volume (the first item, for example, has the largest volume). So stay away from those foods that list sugar in one of the first three positions.

☐ Of course, excessive sugar is not the only culprit in the typical American diet. Excessive salt is also a problem, as well as too many fried foods and foods lacking in natural fiber. Many good books are available that explain the basics of good nutrition. A wealth of ideas and menus for nutritious snacks and brown bag lunches can be found in Vicki Lansky's book *The Taming of the C.A.N.D.Y. Monster (Continuously Advertised Nutritionally Deficient Yummies)*—an inexpensive paperback from Meadowbrook Press. Other good sources of nutrition information and healthy recipes are Yvonne Baker's books *From God's Natural Storehouse* and *Guilt-Free Snacking* (both from David C. Cook).

Good nutrition, however, is only half the story. Adequate exercise is essential as well. While most young children don't have to be encouraged to be active, recent studies of overweight children indicate that in a great majority of cases, the problem is directly related to inadequate exercise. As children get older, they need encouragement to maintain a healthy level of physical conditioning. Here's where your lead is critical.

☐ Build happy family times and memories around both energetic physical work and good physical exercise. Take frequent walks or bicycle rides, or run or jog as a family. Play sports that get the pulse rate up for a conditioning effect. Take a look at Dr. Kenneth Cooper's excellent book *The Aerobics Program for Total Well-Being* (Bantam). See especially the chapter on the aerobic family.

☐ Familiarize yourself with the school physical education program. Most are structured as a succession of units featuring various kinds of skills and exercises. Try them at home as a family, letting your youngster take the lead.

☐ Encourage your youngster's participation in individual and team sports. Keep the focus off winning and on the mental attitude of doing one's best. When appropriate, provide lessons in the sport, or help your child participate in summer recreation programs where he or she will receive good instruction and encouragement.

☐ If your child is small, encourage his or her natural desire to play and wrestle on the floor with you. Betty May's book

167

T.S.K.H. * *(Tickle, Snug, Kiss, Hug)* (Paulist Press) has a wealth of exercises and tricks for parent-child fun.

☐ Don't overlook the importance to health of adequate rest. Make sure your child understands the consequences of staying up late when he or she has to rise early the next morning for school. Help the child observe a firm schedule for bedtime on school nights.

☐ Discuss the need for dressing properly with regard to the weather. Help your young child see the connection between getting chilled and becoming vulnerable to illness.

Through it all, maintain a balanced approach and sense of humor. Changing family eating or exercise patterns isn't easy. Talk together about your goals and try to avoid the sharp pendulum swings so typical of diet and exercise fads. A gradual transition into new habits rather than a sudden, radical change will improve your chances for success and prompt less protest from your child. Meanwhile, focus on the lifetime benefits you and your family will enjoy as you make the commitment together to healthful living.

38

YOUR CHILD CAN LOVE TO LEARN

WOULD it surprise you to learn that research reveals a strong and direct relationship between parents' involvement with their children and the kids' achievements in school? It shouldn't. Yet many parents tend to let teachers carry the full burden of their children's education. Somehow many parents harbor a vague notion that only professional educators can adequately evaluate a child's progress. But nothing could be further from the truth!

If you sincerely believe that teaching your child to value school and the learning process is one of the most important gifts you can give, you must get involved. Here are some ways:

☐ With a preschooler, the critical focus is to build a strong sense of self-worth and the knowledge that the child is loved and accepted for himself. From this secure foundation, your child can explore the new world of people, things, and ideas to which he or she will be exposed.

☐ Listen to your child. Your genuine excitement over your child's interests and discoveries is essential to helping him or her learn that exploration and discovery are both fun and important.

☐ Consistently read to your child from a variety of sources. Listen to records and play together with toys that prompt creative interaction. Also let your preschooler observe you solving problems and tracking down information.

☐ This is the age to introduce your child to the riches of the public library. Ask your librarian to recommend some good books. Check out copies of the Caldecott Award winners (presented to the best picture books in America each year).

Find out what programs are available for youngsters— most libraries have story times, puppet shows, films, and other regular or special events. Take advantage of nonprint materials the library might offer for checkout, such as phonograph records of stories, finger plays or music, or framed prints to hang in your child's room. He or she will soon get the idea that learning is fun and rewarding, and this conviction will be established for life.

☐ If your child is in an early elementary grade, your participation at school events is most important. Take the time to meet your child's teacher and ask direct questions about his or her educational philosophy and approach to teaching. Ask what special activity or project you could help with. And seek time off from your job if necessary to help in the classroom twice a year. Make sure you show up at parent-teacher conferences, open house, school programs, and even some P.T.A. or school board meetings.

☐ From your child's teacher, obtain a copy of the basic weekly class schedule and the themes that will be taught each week. This will help you to avoid questions such as "What did you do in school today?" and the common "Aw, nothing" response.

☐ Ask your child to read to you from books, newspaper or magazine articles, menus, and signs. Let him or her know it helps you when he or she shares something interesting or informative. Dig into dictionaries together whenever an interesting new word comes up in conversation.

☐ Stimulate math and language skills by playing Scrabble, Dominoes, Monopoly, and the like. While traveling in the car or waiting in line, challenge your child to word games and rhyme making.

☐ Explore a book of world records or trivia together—both are favorites with kids. Have trivia contests around the dinner table, or let a family member give a report each week on something he or she has learned from a book or TV.

☐ Periodic visits to local historical sites, factories, museums, concerts, plays—even fire and police stations—are helpful in stimulating a love for learning and exploration. Don't forget the local water treatment plant!

☐ During the late elementary grades your focus will likely shift a bit from cultivating a desire for learning to a stronger emphasis on the constructive use of time. Help your child think through priorities and set goals. Guard against too many good things overtaxing his or her energy and enthusiasm.

☐ Provide your child with a quiet, comfortable, well-lit place to study. Equip it with the basics, such as a dictionary, an atlas or globe, and a pencil sharpener.

☐ Maintain a pattern of learning together by reading books of common interest. Discuss together newspaper articles or TV news. When you perform some task or assembly, let your child read the directions. Praise accomplishments and help him or her understand what can be done to overcome weaknesses. Offer to go along on school field trips.

☐ At the junior and senior high levels, use everything you know about what motivates your child to keep him or her encouraged and moving in the right direction. Share adult conversation with your teenager. Once in a while, take him or her to work with you. You might even consider offering to speak in the young person's classroom on an interesting aspect of your job.

☐ Without pushing, remain a "pal" to your child, and let him or her know you're always there to lend a hand with a difficult assignment or just to talk. Take an active interest in the people and places that consume the bulk of your child's time.

While your child's enjoyment of school and commitment to the value of learning may expand or shrink with varying teachers or learning environments, these are only second in importance to your own influence and modeling. With lifelong patterns of growth and achievement at stake, no amount of effort is too great. In the words of one slogan, "A mind is a terrible thing to waste."

39

WHERE DO KIDS GET CLOSE FAMILY FEELINGS?

UNDERLYING many of the important values you want your child to absorb is one so basic it often escapes notice. Yet in our rootless, transient culture, this critical value is undergoing extensive erosion. It's the value of family—that incredible laboratory where life makes up its mind.

Dr. Harold M. Voth, senior psychiatrist and psychoanalyst at

173

the Menninger Foundation, observes, "The most serious crisis facing us today is that of the family, the alterations of its internal structure, the high incidence of its dissolution, and the associated crisis of the human spirit."

Will your child leave home with an unshakable commitment to fidelity in marriage and to the nuclear family model? The answer will be fashioned directly by your leadership in the family of which he or she is now a part. And three important principles will need to be part of his or her convictions about the family:

- The concept of family is fundamental to God's design for mankind. When it's artificially altered, both society and individuals suffer and fall prey to a host of psychological ills and sociological diseases. In addition, God the Father's authorship of family gives fatherhood an inherent promise and responsibility. In fact, the New Testament Greek word for family is *patria*, which means "fatherhood."
- The family unit is the foundation of individual security, identity, and connectedness. It's the best vehicle through which values and a sense of purpose and destiny can be transmitted. Without a sense of heritage and worth originating in the family, a profound crisis in personal identity is inevitable. No other institution can adequately replace the family. As historian Will Durant has observed, "The family can exist without the state, but without the family all is lost."
- Modeling is the primary way values and personal identity are transmitted in the family. If one grows up outside a traditional family unit, it is almost always difficult to establish a successful family in the next generation.

Here, then, are some ways to enhance the heritage and commitments your child will gain from life in your family:

☐ Talk about the distinctives and values to which your family is committed. Stress them through your conduct. Perhaps you could symbolize them in a family crest, displayed in a prominent spot. As these values are challenged from outside the family, rally together in mutual support.

174

☐ Stress family unity through activities and enjoyable hobbies in which every family member can participate. Build family traditions around these. Make matching family T-shirts or buttons that symbolize your unity and spirit.

☐ Take lots of pictures of your family in action together. Bring them out frequently for review. Make a family scrapbook of nonphoto items that will also help you reminisce about family outings, achievements, and crises faced together. Frequently recite and praise the accomplishments and growth of family members as you review the albums and scrapbook together.

☐ Do some joint research into your family history. Use the genealogical section of your local library and talk with older relatives. Create a family tree and collect old family photos and artifacts.

☐ Write together a contemporary, ongoing history of your own family. You might begin with your marriage and include memorable family occasions up to the present. Write a biographical sketch of each family member that reflects his or her special traits, skills, and talents.

☐ Try to find out the meaning of your family name, as well as the meaning of each member's first and middle name. Books with such information are usually available at the local library.

☐ Make a habit of recording in a special notebook the funny, profound, or otherwise memorable sayings of each child.

☐ Keep in touch with relatives on both sides of your family. Include visits with them at holiday and vacation times. Keep a round-robin family newsletter circulating, and when it comes, gather the family to read it and enjoy the enclosed snapshots. Make a wall display or bulletin board of old family photos including as many relatives as possible.

☐ Periodically stage a family reunion. Emphasize accepting all family members just as they are, including the "black sheep," if any. Fill the time with talent shows, skits that relive episodes in the lives of family members and ancestors, and prizes for the oldest, youngest, worst dressed, tallest, or anything else you can think of. Plan plenty of time for older family members to speak of their past. Take a group photograph and work on charting a family tree. Have everyone bring old photos and family artifacts to share.

☐ If your family has been broken by death or divorce, work at keeping alive every positive connection and look for other individuals, couples, or families with which a surrogate family bond can be built. If grandparents live far away, allow your kids to adopt older friends who live nearby as another set of grandparents.

☐ As much as possible, resist our society's tendency to separate people into age groups. This practice eliminates the interaction needed to pass along traditional values and cultural continuity across generations. Our moral and cultural chaos today is probably at least in part a reflection of this profound loss.

Will your child leave home with a firm commitment to family? It's up to you. In the words of Dr. Voth, "If all goes well, the effects of family life can evoke the best that Nature has to give; if not, family life can have disastrous consequences."

40

GIVE YOUR CHILD A HEART FOR GOD

WHAT will it take to give your child a mature and passionate love for God? After all, it is God's design that parents be responsible to communicate true spiritual values to their children. So the answer starts with you.

What are you modeling on the stage of family life? Timothy's sincere faith first dwelt in his grandmother, Lois, and his mother, Eunice (2 Tim. 1:5). Your children won't catch something you don't have. In fact, if your spiritual life is weak it will only immunize them from catching the real thing.

Paul's words in 2 Timothy 3:14, 15 indicate that our real goal is the third of three stages. The first is *knowledge* (reliable information about God). The second is *learning* (personal application of those truths). And the third is *wisdom* (a pattern of seeing from God's point of view). Parents who are successful at helping their children arrive at stage three are generally active in several key areas. Let's first take a personal inventory and then look at some practical suggestions.

- Is my own spiritual life worth imitating? Do I pray privately as an intercessor for the specific needs of my family?
- Do I have a natural enthusiasm for spiritual things, or are prayer, Bible study, and church activities merely rote or optional habits?
- Is my discipline of my child creating in him or her a balanced respect for authority that will help the child willingly respond to God's authority?
- Do I take my child to the Scriptures to discuss his or her problems, positive character traits being acquired, world events that concern the child, or questions about life?
- Is prayer joined with action my natural response when my child comes to me with needs? Does he or she see me take problems before God first? Does our family pray together naturally and spontaneously at other than mealtimes or bedtimes?

Psychological studies indicate that about 85 percent of your child's adult personality has been formed by his or her sixth birthday. So your best chance for success is to love and discipline your child effectively during those first crucial years. Then, as you work on the remaining 15 percent, here are some suggestions:

☐ If you've never consecrated your child to God by name, do it now. Give your child to him and recognize that he or she is only in your keeping for a season.

☐ Pray for your child daily. Stay aware of his or her specific needs so that you can pray specifically. Let the child know you pray for him or her. Be sure to point out God's answers to prayer in the child's life. Pray often for his or her future concerns as well, such as vocations, spouse, and children.

☐ Build a balanced climate in your home of laughter, adventure, surprises, mutual care, good music and books, and good friends. Make it fun to live there. One test of your home's climate is whether the neighborhood kids like to congregate there!

☐ Have frequent times of spiritual interaction as a family, tailored to the interests and attention span of your child. Get him or her involved in contributing. Change the pace frequently. Reward the child for memorizing Scripture.

☐ Have times of spontaneous family worship. When a happy event calls for celebration, thank God in songs and prayer together.

☐ Involve your kid in an effective Christian summer camping program and any good scouting or youth program your church sponsors.

☐ Treat your child's questions about spiritual matters seriously. Don't laugh if he or she wants to know if mosquitoes go to heaven; use the question as a chance to talk about our promised eternal life in God's presence. If you don't know an answer, say so; then go to the Bible together for further insight.

☐ Take advantage of holidays and other special occasions to talk about your faith. What better time to discuss God's love for mankind than on Christmas Eve, or his power than on Easter morning? Even birthdays can become occasions for emphasizing the uniqueness and worth in God's eyes of the person being honored, and wedding anniversaries are a natural time to discuss God's plan for marriages.

☐ Help your child become familiar and comfortable with your church—its members, order of worship, and activities.

☐ Expose your child to biographies of great Christian men and women and to contemporary Christian music with a message.

☐ Hang a world map on your wall and study regularly the areas of hunger, political repression, and spiritual need. Write to missions groups for materials that tell what God is doing in various countries.

☐ Invite missionaries and spiritually committed people into

your home. Encourage your child to ask questions to learn how God called these people.

☐ On a family bulletin board, post pictures of missionaries you have met. Correspond with them. Pray and give as a family to help meet their needs.

☐ On your family vacation visit a missions outreach or inner city ministry in the area where you're going.

☐ Identify friends of your child who do not know Christ. Pray and plan ways to spend time with them that might become an opportunity to share the gospel message. Make sure you and your child know what to say when the opportunity arises.

☐ During your child's teenage years, his or her faith must become able to stand independently from yours. A teenager will likely begin questioning much of what he or she has previously accepted. Don't panic. Pray and provide exposure both to literature that gives solid answers to his or her questions, and to speakers who communicate well with young people. Be open to calm discussion yourself, and more than ever, practice what you preach.

In Proverbs 22:6, God promises you can give your child a heart for him. It's an ongoing process of mutual growth each day that will have immediate joys—and eternal rewards.

A P P E N D I X
KEEPING TRACK

Child's name _____

Current age _____

Date of this record update _____

√ = Current Area of Focus   (Circle Current Status)

✗ = Successful Performance

SKILLS: Poor   Great

1. _____ Allowances and financial
responsibility   1 2 3 4 5 6 7 8 9 10

2. _____ Making good decisions   1 2 3 4 5 6 7 8 9 10

3. _____ Finding and managing time   1 2 3 4 5 6 7 8 9 10

4. _____ The art of friendship   1 2 3 4 5 6 7 8 9 10

5. _____ Understanding politics   1 2 3 4 5 6 7 8 9 10

6. _____ Coping with guilt   1 2 3 4 5 6 7 8 9 10

7. _____ Deciphering hidden
messages   1 2 3 4 5 6 7 8 9 10

8. _____ Understanding finance and
economics   1 2 3 4 5 6 7 8 9 10

9. _____ Giving and receiving
criticism   1 2 3 4 5 6 7 8 9 10

10. _____ Handling stress   1 2 3 4 5 6 7 8 9 10

11. _____ Dealing with death   1 2 3 4 5 6 7 8 9 10

12. _____ Succeeding at love and dating   1 2 3 4 5 6 7 8 9 10

13. _____ Being neat and clean   1 2 3 4 5 6 7 8 9 10

ATTITUDES:

14. _____ A proper view of success   1 2 3 4 5 6 7 8 9 10

15. _____ Chores and responsibility   1 2 3 4 5 6 7 8 9 10

16. _____ Overcoming the fear of failure   1 2 3 4 5 6 7 8 9 10

17. _____ Self-esteem   1 2 3 4 5 6 7 8 9 10

18. _____ A thankful spirit   1 2 3 4 5 6 7 8 9 10
19. _____ Creativity   1 2 3 4 5 6 7 8 9 10
20. _____ A "can do" spirit   1 2 3 4 5 6 7 8 9 10
21. _____ The art of serving   1 2 3 4 5 6 7 8 9 10
22. _____ Laughing matters   1 2 3 4 5 6 7 8 9 10
23. _____ Kicking the blues   1 2 3 4 5 6 7 8 9 10
24. _____ Learning to follow through   1 2 3 4 5 6 7 8 9 10
25. _____ A positive view of authority   1 2 3 4 5 6 7 8 9 10
26. _____ Respecting simplicity   1 2 3 4 5 6 7 8 9 10

VALUES:

27. _____ Honesty   1 2 3 4 5 6 7 8 9 10
28. _____ Discernment with TV   1 2 3 4 5 6 7 8 9 10
29. _____ Learning about sex   1 2 3 4 5 6 7 8 9 10
30. _____ Kids' rights   1 2 3 4 5 6 7 8 9 10
31. _____ Family traditions   1 2 3 4 5 6 7 8 9 10
32. _____ The value of things   1 2 3 4 5 6 7 8 9 10
33. _____ Family roots   1 2 3 4 5 6 7 8 9 10
34. _____ Respecting privacy   1 2 3 4 5 6 7 8 9 10
35. _____ Courage   1 2 3 4 5 6 7 8 9 10
36. _____ A thirst for the arts   1 2 3 4 5 6 7 8 9 10
37. _____ Good health habits   1 2 3 4 5 6 7 8 9 10
38. _____ The value of learning   1 2 3 4 5 6 7 8 9 10
39. _____ Commitment to family   1 2 3 4 5 6 7 8 9 10
40. _____ A heart for God   1 2 3 4 5 6 7 8 9 10

Child's name _____

Current age _____

Date of this record update _____

√ = Current Area of Focus   (Circle Current Status)

X = Successful Performance

SKILLS:

	Poor									Great
1. ____ Allowances and financial responsibility	1	2	3	4	5	6	7	8	9	10
2. ____ Making good decisions	1	2	3	4	5	6	7	8	9	10
3. ____ Finding and managing time	1	2	3	4	5	6	7	8	9	10
4. ____ The art of friendship	1	2	3	4	5	6	7	8	9	10
5. ____ Understanding politics	1	2	3	4	5	6	7	8	9	10
6. ____ Coping with guilt	1	2	3	4	5	6	7	8	9	10
7. ____ Deciphering hidden messages	1	2	3	4	5	6	7	8	9	10
8. ____ Understanding finance and economics	1	2	3	4	5	6	7	8	9	10
9. ____ Giving and receiving criticism	1	2	3	4	5	6	7	8	9	10
10. ____ Handling stress	1	2	3	4	5	6	7	8	9	10
11. ____ Dealing with death	1	2	3	4	5	6	7	8	9	10
12. ____ Succeeding at love and dating	1	2	3	4	5	6	7	8	9	10
13. ____ Being neat and clean	1	2	3	4	5	6	7	8	9	10

ATTITUDES:

14. ____ A proper view of success	1	2	3	4	5	6	7	8	9	10
15. ____ Chores and responsibility	1	2	3	4	5	6	7	8	9	10
16. ____ Overcoming the fear of failure	1	2	3	4	5	6	7	8	9	10
17. ____ Self-esteem	1	2	3	4	5	6	7	8	9	10

18. _____ A thankful spirit   1 2 3 4 5 6 7 8 9 10
19. _____ Creativity   1 2 3 4 5 6 7 8 9 10
20. _____ A "can do" spirit   1 2 3 4 5 6 7 8 9 10
21. _____ The art of serving   1 2 3 4 5 6 7 8 9 10
22. _____ Laughing matters   1 2 3 4 5 6 7 8 9 10
23. _____ Kicking the blues   1 2 3 4 5 6 7 8 9 10
24. _____ Learning to follow through   1 2 3 4 5 6 7 8 9 10
25. _____ A positive view of authority   1 2 3 4 5 6 7 8 9 10
26. _____ Respecting simplicity   1 2 3 4 5 6 7 8 9 10

VALUES:

27. _____ Honesty   1 2 3 4 5 6 7 8 9 10
28. _____ Discernment with TV   1 2 3 4 5 6 7 8 9 10
29. _____ Learning about sex   1 2 3 4 5 6 7 8 9 10
30. _____ Kids' rights   1 2 3 4 5 6 7 8 9 10
31. _____ Family traditions   1 2 3 4 5 6 7 8 9 10
32. _____ The value of things   1 2 3 4 5 6 7 8 9 10
33. _____ Family roots   1 2 3 4 5 6 7 8 9 10
34. _____ Respecting privacy   1 2 3 4 5 6 7 8 9 10
35. _____ Courage   1 2 3 4 5 6 7 8 9 10
36. _____ A thirst for the arts   1 2 3 4 5 6 7 8 9 10
37. _____ Good health habits   1 2 3 4 5 6 7 8 9 10
38. _____ The value of learning   1 2 3 4 5 6 7 8 9 10
39. _____ Commitment to family   1 2 3 4 5 6 7 8 9 10
40. _____ A heart for God   1 2 3 4 5 6 7 8 9 10

Child's name _____

Current age _____

Date of this record update _____

√ = Current Area of Focus   (Circle Current Status)

X = Successful Performance

SKILLS:

		Poor									Great
1. ____	Allowances and financial responsibility	1	2	3	4	5	6	7	8	9	10
2. ____	Making good decisions	1	2	3	4	5	6	7	8	9	10
3. ____	Finding and managing time	1	2	3	4	5	6	7	8	9	10
4. ____	The art of friendship	1	2	3	4	5	6	7	8	9	10
5. ____	Understanding politics	1	2	3	4	5	6	7	8	9	10
6. ____	Coping with guilt	1	2	3	4	5	6	7	8	9	10
7. ____	Deciphering hidden messages	1	2	3	4	5	6	7	8	9	10
8. ____	Understanding finance and economics	1	2	3	4	5	6	7	8	9	10
9. ____	Giving and receiving criticism	1	2	3	4	5	6	7	8	9	10
10. ____	Handling stress	1	2	3	4	5	6	7	8	9	10
11. ____	Dealing with death	1	2	3	4	5	6	7	8	9	10
12. ____	Succeeding at love and dating	1	2	3	4	5	6	7	8	9	10
13. ____	Being neat and clean	1	2	3	4	5	6	7	8	9	10

ATTITUDES:

14. ____	A proper view of success	1	2	3	4	5	6	7	8	9	10
15. ____	Chores and responsibility	1	2	3	4	5	6	7	8	9	10
16. ____	Overcoming the fear of failure	1	2	3	4	5	6	7	8	9	10
17. ____	Self-esteem	1	2	3	4	5	6	7	8	9	10

18. _____ A thankful spirit   1 2 3 4 5 6 7 8 9 10
19. _____ Creativity   1 2 3 4 5 6 7 8 9 10
20. _____ A "can do" spirit   1 2 3 4 5 6 7 8 9 10
21. _____ The art of serving   1 2 3 4 5 6 7 8 9 10
22. _____ Laughing matters   1 2 3 4 5 6 7 8 9 10
23. _____ Kicking the blues   1 2 3 4 5 6 7 8 9 10
24. _____ Learning to follow through 1 2 3 4 5 6 7 8 9 10
25. _____ A positive view of authority 1 2 3 4 5 6 7 8 9 10
26. _____ Respecting simplicity   1 2 3 4 5 6 7 8 9 10

VALUES:

27. _____ Honesty   1 2 3 4 5 6 7 8 9 10
28. _____ Discernment with TV   1 2 3 4 5 6 7 8 9 10
29. _____ Learning about sex   1 2 3 4 5 6 7 8 9 10
30. _____ Kids' rights   1 2 3 4 5 6 7 8 9 10
31. _____ Family traditions   1 2 3 4 5 6 7 8 9 10
32. _____ The value of things   1 2 3 4 5 6 7 8 9 10
33. _____ Family roots   1 2 3 4 5 6 7 8 9 10
34. _____ Respecting privacy   1 2 3 4 5 6 7 8 9 10
35. _____ Courage   1 2 3 4 5 6 7 8 9 10
36. _____ A thirst for the arts   1 2 3 4 5 6 7 8 9 10
37. _____ Good health habits   1 2 3 4 5 6 7 8 9 10
38. _____ The value of learning   1 2 3 4 5 6 7 8 9 10
39. _____ Commitment to family   1 2 3 4 5 6 7 8 9 10
40. _____ A heart for God   1 2 3 4 5 6 7 8 9 10

Child's name _____

Current age _____

Date of this record update _____

√ = Current Area of Focus   (Circle Current Status)

Ҳ = Successful Performance

SKILLS: Poor   Great

1. _____ Allowances and financial
         responsibility   1 2 3 4 5 6 7 8 9 10

2. _____ Making good decisions   1 2 3 4 5 6 7 8 9 10

3. _____ Finding and managing time 1 2 3 4 5 6 7 8 9 10

4. _____ The art of friendship   1 2 3 4 5 6 7 8 9 10

5. _____ Understanding politics   1 2 3 4 5 6 7 8 9 10

6. _____ Coping with guilt   1 2 3 4 5 6 7 8 9 10

7. _____ Deciphering hidden
         messages   1 2 3 4 5 6 7 8 9 10

8. _____ Understanding finance and
         economics   1 2 3 4 5 6 7 8 9 10

9. _____ Giving and receiving
         criticism   1 2 3 4 5 6 7 8 9 10

10. _____ Handling stress   1 2 3 4 5 6 7 8 9 10

11. _____ Dealing with death   1 2 3 4 5 6 7 8 9 10

12. _____ Succeeding at love and dating 1 2 3 4 5 6 7 8 9 10

13. _____ Being neat and clean   1 2 3 4 5 6 7 8 9 10

ATTITUDES:

14. _____ A proper view of success 1 2 3 4 5 6 7 8 9 10

15. _____ Chores and responsibility 1 2 3 4 5 6 7 8 9 10

16. _____ Overcoming the fear of failure 1 2 3 4 5 6 7 8 9 10

17. _____ Self-esteem   1 2 3 4 5 6 7 8 9 10

18. _____ A thankful spirit	1	2	3	4	5	6	7	8	9	10
19. _____ Creativity	1	2	3	4	5	6	7	8	9	10
20. _____ A "can do" spirit	1	2	3	4	5	6	7	8	9	10
21. _____ The art of serving	1	2	3	4	5	6	7	8	9	10
22. _____ Laughing matters	1	2	3	4	5	6	7	8	9	10
23. _____ Kicking the blues	1	2	3	4	5	6	7	8	9	10
24. _____ Learning to follow through	1	2	3	4	5	6	7	8	9	10
25. _____ A positive view of authority	1	2	3	4	5	6	7	8	9	10
26. _____ Respecting simplicity	1	2	3	4	5	6	7	8	9	10

VALUES:

27. _____ Honesty	1	2	3	4	5	6	7	8	9	10
28. _____ Discernment with TV	1	2	3	4	5	6	7	8	9	10
29. _____ Learning about sex	1	2	3	4	5	6	7	8	9	10
30. _____ Kids' rights	1	2	3	4	5	6	7	8	9	10
31. _____ Family traditions	1	2	3	4	5	6	7	8	9	10
32. _____ The value of things	1	2	3	4	5	6	7	8	9	10
33. _____ Family roots	1	2	3	4	5	6	7	8	9	10
34. _____ Respecting privacy	1	2	3	4	5	6	7	8	9	10
35. _____ Courage	1	2	3	4	5	6	7	8	9	10
36. _____ A thirst for the arts	1	2	3	4	5	6	7	8	9	10
37. _____ Good health habits	1	2	3	4	5	6	7	8	9	10
38. _____ The value of learning	1	2	3	4	5	6	7	8	9	10
39. _____ Commitment to family	1	2	3	4	5	6	7	8	9	10
40. _____ A heart for God	1	2	3	4	5	6	7	8	9	10

Child's name _____

Current age _____

Date of this record update _____

√ = Current Area of Focus   (Circle Current Status)

X = Successful Performance

SKILLS: Poor   Great

1. _____ Allowances and financial
responsibility   1 2 3 4 5 6 7 8 9 10

2. _____ Making good decisions   1 2 3 4 5 6 7 8 9 10

3. _____ Finding and managing time   1 2 3 4 5 6 7 8 9 10

4. _____ The art of friendship   1 2 3 4 5 6 7 8 9 10

5. _____ Understanding politics   1 2 3 4 5 6 7 8 9 10

6. _____ Coping with guilt   1 2 3 4 5 6 7 8 9 10

7. _____ Deciphering hidden
messages   1 2 3 4 5 6 7 8 9 10

8. _____ Understanding finance and
economics   1 2 3 4 5 6 7 8 9 10

9. _____ Giving and receiving
criticism   1 2 3 4 5 6 7 8 9 10

10. _____ Handling stress   1 2 3 4 5 6 7 8 9 10

11. _____ Dealing with death   1 2 3 4 5 6 7 8 9 10

12. _____ Succeeding at love and dating   1 2 3 4 5 6 7 8 9 10

13. _____ Being neat and clean   1 2 3 4 5 6 7 8 9 10

ATTITUDES:

14. _____ A proper view of success   1 2 3 4 5 6 7 8 9 10

15. _____ Chores and responsibility   1 2 3 4 5 6 7 8 9 10

16. _____ Overcoming the fear of failure   1 2 3 4 5 6 7 8 9 10

17. _____ Self-esteem   1 2 3 4 5 6 7 8 9 10

18. _____ A thankful spirit   1 2 3 4 5 6 7 8 9 10

19. _____ Creativity   1 2 3 4 5 6 7 8 9 10

20. _____ A "can do" spirit   1 2 3 4 5 6 7 8 9 10

21. _____ The art of serving   1 2 3 4 5 6 7 8 9 10

22. _____ Laughing matters   1 2 3 4 5 6 7 8 9 10

23. _____ Kicking the blues   1 2 3 4 5 6 7 8 9 10

24. _____ Learning to follow through   1 2 3 4 5 6 7 8 9 10

25. _____ A positive view of authority   1 2 3 4 5 6 7 8 9 10

26. _____ Respecting simplicity   1 2 3 4 5 6 7 8 9 10

VALUES:

27. _____ Honesty   1 2 3 4 5 6 7 8 9 10

28. _____ Discernment with TV   1 2 3 4 5 6 7 8 9 10

29. _____ Learning about sex   1 2 3 4 5 6 7 8 9 10

30. _____ Kids' rights   1 2 3 4 5 6 7 8 9 10

31. _____ Family traditions   1 2 3 4 5 6 7 8 9 10

32. _____ The value of things   1 2 3 4 5 6 7 8 9 10

33. _____ Family roots   1 2 3 4 5 6 7 8 9 10

34. _____ Respecting privacy   1 2 3 4 5 6 7 8 9 10

35. _____ Courage   1 2 3 4 5 6 7 8 9 10

36. _____ A thirst for the arts   1 2 3 4 5 6 7 8 9 10

37. _____ Good health habits   1 2 3 4 5 6 7 8 9 10

38. _____ The value of learning   1 2 3 4 5 6 7 8 9 10

39. _____ Commitment to family   1 2 3 4 5 6 7 8 9 10

40. _____ A heart for God   1 2 3 4 5 6 7 8 9 10

DADS ONLY Editor, **PAUL LEWIS**, invites you to join the thousands of fathers across America who read

DADS ONLY NEWSLETTER...
Every month, 12-pages of the quick tips and ideas you need to stay "famous" with your kids!

Clip and mail to: **DADS ONLY, P.O. Box 340, Julian, CA 92036**

SPECIAL SUBSCRIPTION OFFER
for "40 WAYS" Readers

NINE Monthly Issues—Only $10.97

☐ Please enter my subscription to DADS ONLY. I accept your **UNCONDITIONAL GUARANTEE** that I must be completely satisfied that the ideas and advice in DADS ONLY will make a difference in my family, or the entire subscription price will be refunded. I can't lose!

_____
Subscriber's Name

_____
Mailing Address

_____
City/State/Zip

☐ This is a gift subscription. My name and address are attached. Please send a gift card

Check One: CEV

☐ Bill Me

☐ My payment is enclosed—
   add a **BONUS ISSUE** to my term!

☐ Charge my ☐ VISA ☐ MasterCard
No. _____

Chuck Swindoll says:
"Face it, dads, we've got some challenge. If you're like me, you could use a regular dose of ideas, dispensed monthly into your head. DADS ONLY does that. Go for it!